The New York Times

Will Shortz Presents

KENKEN™

The New York Times

WILL SHORTZ PRESENTS
KENKEN™

300 EASY TO HARD PUZZLES
THAT MAKE YOU SMARTER

TETSUYA MIYAMOTO

INTRODUCTION BY
WILL SHORTZ

ST. MARTIN'S GRIFFIN
NEW YORK

www.stmartins.com

ISBN-13: 978-0-312-60321-2
ISBN-10: 0-312-60321-5

10   9   8   7   6   5

Introduction

If you consider all the world's greatest puzzle varieties, the ones that have inspired crazes over the years—crosswords, jigsaw puzzles, tangrams, sudoku, etc.—they have several properties in common. They . . .

- Are simple to learn
- Have great depth
- Are variable in difficulty, from easy to hard
- Are mentally soothing and pleasing
- Have some unique feature that makes them different from everything else and instantly addictive

By these standards, a new puzzle called KenKen, the subject of the book you're holding, has the potential to become one of the world's greats.

KenKen is Japanese for "square wisdom" or "cleverness squared." The rules are simple: Fill the grid with digits so as not to repeat a digit in any row or column (as in sudoku) and so the digits within each heavily outlined group of boxes combine to make the arithmetic result indicated.

The simplest KenKen puzzles start with 3×3 boxes and use only addition. Harder examples have larger grids and more arithmetic operations.

KenKen was invented in 2003 by Tetsuya Miyamoto, a Japanese math instructor, as a means to help his students learn arithmetic and develop logical thinking. Tetsuya's education method is unusual. Put simply, he doesn't teach.

His philosophy is to make the tools of learning available to students and then let them progress on their own.

Tetsuya's most popular learning tool has been KenKen, which his students spend hours doing and find more engaging than TV and video games.

It's true that KenKen has great capacity for educating and building the mind. But first and foremost it's a puzzle to be enjoyed. It is to numbers what the crossword puzzle is to words.

So turn the page and begin. . . .

—Will Shortz

How to Solve KenKen

KenKen is a logic puzzle with simple rules:

- Fill the grid with digits so as not to repeat a digit in any row or column.
- Digits within each heavily outlined group of squares, called a cage, must combine to make the arithmetic result indicated.
- A 3×3–square puzzle will use the digits from 1 to 3, a 4×4–square puzzle will use the digits from 1 to 4, etc.

Solving a KenKen puzzle involves pure logic and mathematics. No guesswork is needed. Every puzzle has a unique solution.

In this volume of KenKen, the puzzles use all four arithmetic operations—addition, subtraction, multiplication, and division—in the following manner:

- In a cage marked with a plus sign, the given number will be the sum of the digits you enter in the squares.
- In a cage marked with a minus sign, the given number will be the difference between the digits you enter in the squares (the lower digit subtracted from the higher one).

Take the 5 × 5–square example on this page.

48×		**3+**		**4−**
	8+	**10×**	**4+**	
3−				**2÷**
	4+		**4**	
7+			**15×**	

To start, fill in any digits in 1 × 1 sections—in this puzzle, the 4 in the fourth row. These are literally no-brainers.

Next, look for sections whose given numbers are either high or low, or that involve distinctive combinations of digits, since these are often the easiest to solve. For example, the L-shaped group in the upper left has a product of 48. The only combination of three digits from 1 to 5 that multiplies to 48 is 3, 4, and 4. Since the two 4s can't appear in the same row or column, they must appear at the ends of the L. The 3 goes between them.

Now look at the pair of squares in the first row with a sum of 3. The only two digits that add up to 3 are 1 and 2. We don't know their order yet, but this information can still be useful.

Sometimes, the next step in solving a KenKen puzzle is to ignore the given numbers and use sudoku-like logic to avoid repeating a digit in a row or column. For example, now that 1, 2, 3, and 4 have been used or are slated for use in the first row, the remaining square (at the end of the row) must be a 5. Then the digit below the 5 must be a 1 for this pair of squares to have a difference of 4.

Next, consider the pair of squares in the third column with a product of 10. The only two digits from 1 to 5 that have a product of 10 are 2 and 5. We

48× 3	4	3+ 1	2	4− 5
4	8+ 5	10× 2	4+ 3	1
3− 2	3	5	1	2÷ 4
5	4+ 1	3	4 4	2
7+ 1	2	4	15× 5	3

don't know their order yet. However, the digit in the square above them, which we previously identified as either a 1 or a 2, must be 1, so as not to repeat a 2 in this column. The 2 that accompanies the 1 goes to its right.

Continuing in this way, using these and other techniques left for you to discover, you can work your way around the grid, filling in the rest of the squares. The complete solution is shown on page ix.

Additional Tips

- In advanced KenKen puzzles, as you've seen, cages can have more than two squares. It's okay for a cage to repeat a digit—as long as the digit is not repeated in a row or column.
- Cages with more than two squares will always involve addition or multiplication. Subtraction and division occur only in cages with exactly two squares.
- Remember, in doing KenKen, you never have to guess. Every puzzle can be solved by using step-by-step logic. Keep going, and soon you'll be a KenKen master!

The New York Times

Will Shortz Presents

KENKEN™

Easy +/−/×/÷   1

7+	3+	6×	
4	1	3	2
		3−	
3	2	4	1
5+		**1**	**12×**
2	3	1	4
1	**2÷**		
1	1	2	3

4+		3−	2
3	1	4	2
2÷			**12×**
2	4	1	3
3−	**6×**		
1	3	2	4
	2	**4+**	
4	2	3	1

12×		3+	2÷
3	4	1	2
4+			
1	3	2	4
2−	**2**	**4+**	
4	2	3	1
	3−		**3**
2	1	4	3

4 Easy +/−/×/÷

6× 3	**2÷** 4	2	**1** 1
2	**3** 3	**3−** 1	4
3−	**2÷**	**7+** 4	3
3		**6×** 3	

7+ 4	3	2÷ 2	1
2 2	3− 4	1	6× 3
2− 3	1	4 4	2
3+ 1	2	7+ 3	4

6×	3−	12×	
		2	3+
3−	1−		
	2÷		3

5+	2÷	18×	
			3−
5+	4+	3−	
			2

2÷		10+	
3−	9+		
		4×	
12×			1

7+		**3−**	**2÷**
1−			
3−	**2÷**	**2**	**36×**

18×		3−	3+
3−			
	2÷		1−
2÷		3	

7+	2	2−	
	9×		2÷
		8×	
7+			

3+		7+	4
2	3×		6×
1−			
	2÷		

2÷	12×		2−
	3+		
3×	4	1−	2÷

14 Easy +/−/×/÷

2−	7+	1−	
		2÷	
2÷	3+		36×
	1		

Easy +/−/×/÷ 15

2÷	**7+**	**6×**	
			3−
1	**6×**		
4+		**2÷**	

4	7+	2÷	
6×		24×	
	3+		
	3−		3

4+	6×	3−	
		2÷	5+
3−			
24×			1

18 Easy +/−/×/÷

Easy +/−/×/÷ 19

2− 2	**4+** 3	1	**4** 4
4	**3+** 1	**7+** 3 ₄	**6×** 2 ₃
8+ 1	2	4 ₃	3 ₂
3	4	**2÷** 2	1

20 Easy +/−/×/÷

2−		**2−**	
3+		**12×**	
36×			**2÷**
	3+		

Medium +/−/×/÷ 21

2÷ 1	2	1− 4	3
7+ 3	1	2÷ 2	4
2÷ 4	3	3× 1	2 2
2	4 4	3	1

22 Medium +/−/×/÷

1− 1	2	**7+** 4	**1−** 3
2÷ 4	**4+** 1	3	2
2	3	**8×** 1	4
12× 3	4	2	1

Medium +/−/×/÷ 23

2− 4	2	**8+** 3	**1−** 1
2÷ 1	**12×** 3	4	2
2	4	1	**7+** 3
3 3	**3+** 1	2	4

24 Medium +/−/×/÷

3− 4	**3+** 1	2	**1−** 3
1	**2÷** 2	**2−** 3	4
18× 3	4	1	**1−** 2
2	3	**4** 4	1

2	9×	3−	
2	3	1	4 4
3	1	24× 4	2
7+ 1	2÷ 4	2	3
4	2	2− 3	1

16×		7+	
3			5+
1−		3−	
2÷			3

1−		2÷	5+
2	3	4	1
2−			
3	1	2	4
5+	**2÷**	**1**	**18×**
4	2	1	3
1	4	3	2

28 Medium +/−/×/÷

1	9+		
1−		3−	2
2÷			9×
2÷			

Medium +/−/×/÷   29

12×	**2÷**		**1−**
	4+		
6×		**3−**	
	2	**12×**	

8+	8+		
		1−	1
1	9×		2÷
		4	

Medium +/−/×/÷   31

3+	3−	1−	3
			2÷
1−	5+	2×	

4+		2÷	4
2÷	1−		1−
		36×	
2÷			

Medium +/−/×/÷ 33

1−		4×	
2÷			11+
4+	3−		
		3	

34 Medium +/−/×/÷

3−	**2÷**		**3**
	6×		**8×**
2−		**3−**	
5+			

Medium +/−/×/÷   35

1−		11+	
3	**2÷**		
5+	**2÷**	**9×**	

3−	2÷		6+
	1−		
18×	3−		
		5+	

Medium +/−/×/÷   37

2÷		**2−**	
1−	**12×**		**2÷**
	3−		
4+		**2÷**	

8×	2÷		10+
18×	3−		7+

Medium +/−/×/÷   39

7+	3−		4×
	1−		
2÷		1−	
	4	2−	

40 Medium +/−/×/÷

6+	1−		2
	8+		
	2÷		9×
4			

1−		4+	2÷
4×			
	9+		2−
3−			

2−	6+	6×	
			3
2−	2÷		5+
	1−		

12×			2÷
2÷	1	10+	
	1−		
4		1−	

2÷		6×	
3−	6+		
		13+	
2−			

Medium +/−/×/÷ 45

9+		**3−**	
1−		**1−**	
	9×		**2÷**
5+			

46 Medium +/−/×/÷

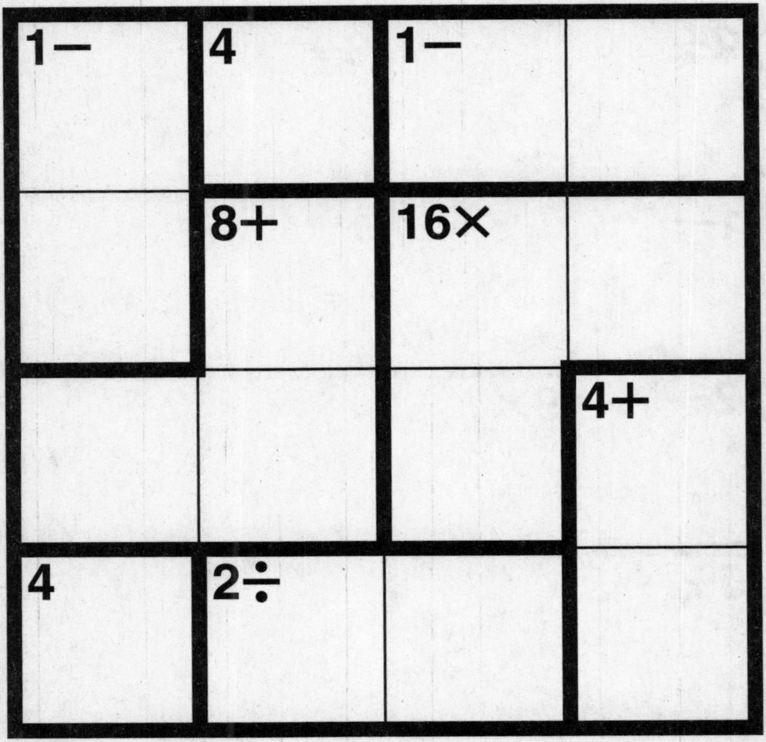

A 4×4 KenKen puzzle grid with the following cage clues:

1−	4	1−	
	8+	16×	
			4+
4	2÷		

Medium +/−/×/÷ 47

2÷	3×		2
	4		1−
2−	1−	7+	

48 Medium +/−/×/÷

3−	72×	2÷	
1−	8+		2÷
	1		

Medium +/−/×/÷ 49

2÷		**10+**	**1−**
12×			
		2−	
2		**2−**	

50 Medium +/−/×/÷

2−	4×		1−
	1−		
2÷		7+	2÷
	1		

Medium +/−/×/÷ 51

5+		**6×**	**2−**
2÷	**1−**		
		8×	
4+		**4**	

52 Medium +/−/×/÷

3−	1	1−	1−
	2÷		
8+		2	4×

Medium +/−/×/÷   53

6×	**2÷**	**5+**	
		16×	
	3		**2−**
8×			

3−	2÷		1−
	12×		
5+	2−	6+	
		3	

Medium +/−/×/÷ 55

2÷	**6×**		
	3	**5+**	
1−		**32×**	**2−**

6×		4+	48×
2÷			
	8+		
		1−	

2÷		10+	
12×	6+	4	
			2÷
	2−		

Medium +/−/×/÷   59

6+	16×		2
	2−		1−
		6×	
2÷			

2÷		9×	
1	1−	3−	
1−			8+
	1		

Medium +/−/×/÷   61

24×	2−		5+
		1−	
3−			1−
1	2÷		

62 Medium +/−/×/÷

2−		**24×**	**3−**
7+			
		1−	
2÷		**4+**	

Medium +/−/×/÷ 63

1−	2÷	2	3−
		9+	
6×			
	3−		3

12×	2÷		4
	3	5+	1−
	7+		
		7+	

Medium +/−/×/÷   65

6×		**2÷**	
3		**6+**	**8+**
3−			
2÷			

66 Medium +/−/×/÷

2÷	12×		
	1−		2−
5+	2−		
		2÷	

3−	1−		9+
	2÷		
12×	4		
		3−	

6×			24×
3−		2÷	
7+	3		
		4+	

Medium +/−/×/÷ 69

12×		**9+**	
2÷		**3−**	
	2÷		**6×**
3			

2÷	6×		1−
	2−	2÷	
12+			2÷

Medium +/−/×/÷　71

2÷ 2	1	**10+** 4	3
8+ 1	4	3	**8×** 2
3	**4×** 2	1	4
1− 4	3	2	1

1−	2−		10+
	2÷		
2÷		6×	
3−			

1−		2÷	3−
48×			
	4+		1−
	2−		

2−		6+	3−
2÷			
7+	3		24×

Medium +/−/×/÷   75

2÷	6×	8+	
2	3	4	1
4	2	**1** 1	3
6+ 3	1	2	**24×** 4
3− 1	4	3	2

2	5+	2÷	6+
12×			
	4+		
	1−		4

3−	24×		
	2	9+	
2÷			3−
1−			

24×		4	6+
	2−		
2÷	8+		
		2÷	

Medium +/−/×/÷ 79

3−		**12×**	**6+**
2÷			
	12×		
3		**5+**	

6+	1−		8×
	16×		
			2−
2÷		3	

Challenging +/−/×/÷ 81

1− 4	3	**8×** 1	**2** 2
2− 3	4	2	**3−** 1 ₄
1	**12+** 2	3	4 ₁
2÷ 2 ₁	1 ₂	4	3

2÷ 2 1	1 2	**1−** 3	4
8+ 1	**7+** 2	4	**6×** 3
3	**4** 4	1	2
4	**1−** 3	2	**1** 1

Challenging +/−/×/÷   83

12×	11+		
3	4	3	2
	1−		**3**
1	2	4	3
		2−	**3−**
4	3	2	1
2÷			
2	1	1	4

84 Challenging +/−/×/÷

2÷	1−		3−
	3	7+	
4	12×		1−

Challenging +/−/×/÷ 85

1−	8×		
	4	2−	
8+		2÷	
	2−		2

2÷		4	12×
1−			
1−	5+	7+	
			1

Challenging +/−/×/÷ 87

2	**12×**		
1−		**2÷**	**7+**
4+			
1−		**1−**	

5+		24×	
2	2−		
8+		2÷	
	2	1−	

Challenging +/−/×/÷ 89

2	**12×**		
5+		**2÷**	**3**
2−			**8×**
1−			

6+	8×		4
		4+	
	9+	1−	
		2÷	

8+	4	1−	
	24×		
	2÷		1−
2÷		3	

24×	2÷	12×	
		5+	
	5+		1−
1	1−		

3−		3	1−
24×	3−		
		2÷	5+
1−			

12×			6+
1−		10+	
1			
2÷		1−	

8×	6+		
	2÷	8+	4
			1−
2−			

1−	5+	6×	
		2÷	
6×			4
2÷		1−	

36×		**1−**	
2÷		**8+**	**9+**
8×			

1−		2÷	
2−		1	24×
2÷	4+		
		1−	

Challenging +/−/×/÷ 99

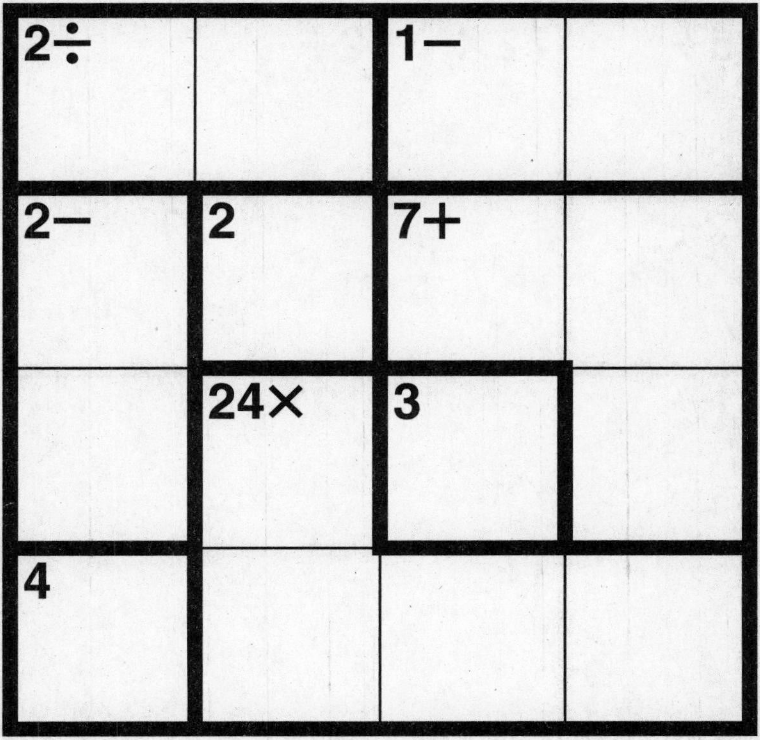

5+	72×	2÷	
			1
1−		12×	
	1−		

Challenging +/−/×/÷ 101

5+		**1−**	
2÷		**4**	**12×**
12×	**1−**		
		1−	

102 Challenging +/−/×/÷

2÷		**8×**	**3**
3			**7+**
1−			
2−		**2−**	

Challenging +/−/×/÷ 103

1−		5+	
1−		1−	2÷
2×	4		
		1−	

2−		8×	
7+	1−		
	2÷	6+	
		3	

Challenging +/−/×/÷ 105

2÷	48×		
	1−		3
8+		1−	2−

12×		1−	
2÷		1−	2÷
	1−		
4		4+	

3−		18×	
2÷		2÷	
2−	9+		5+

108 Challenging +/−/×/÷

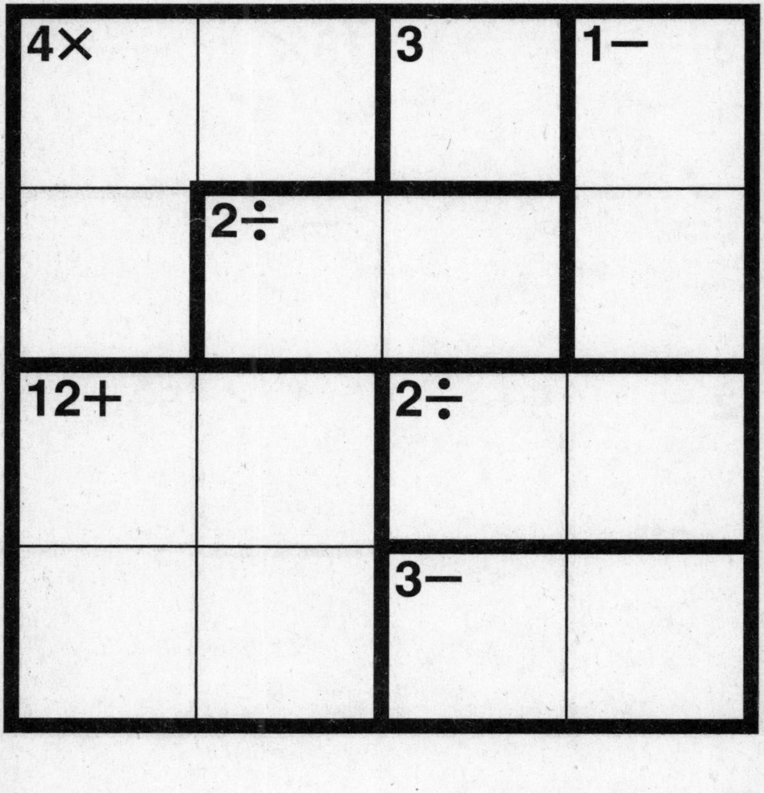

12×		1−	
	3	9+	
2÷	1−	1	
		1−	

24×			5+
4+		1−	
9+			1−
	2÷		

Challenging +/−/×/÷ 111

4×		9+	3
	24×		
1−			2÷
	3−		

8+	2−		8×
	2÷		
		6+	
1−			4

Challenging +/−/×/÷ 113

1	6×		2÷
1−	9+		
		1−	2−

8×		1−	
	4+		2÷
1−		2÷	
1−			1

116 Challenging +/−/×/÷

1−		**2−**	**8×**
12×			
4		**9+**	
2÷			

1−		1−	
1−		2÷	3−
12×			
4		5+	

1−		1−	
8+		8×	
16×		2÷	
			3

Challenging +/−/×/÷ 119

1−	4+		3−
	2÷		
2÷		24×	
1−			

Challenging +/−/×/÷ 121

4+		2÷	
2÷		2−	12×
1−	2−		
		2	

3−	2÷		2−
	1−		
6×	2−	5+	
		2÷	

1−	1−		1
	8×		
2÷		2−	
5+		1−	

1−		2÷	
5+	8×		
	6+		1−
3−			

Challenging +/−/×/÷ 125

1−		**24×**	
6+			**5+**
2÷			
	24×		

1−	12+		
	3	6×	
2÷			
1−		1−	

Challenging +/–/×/÷ 127

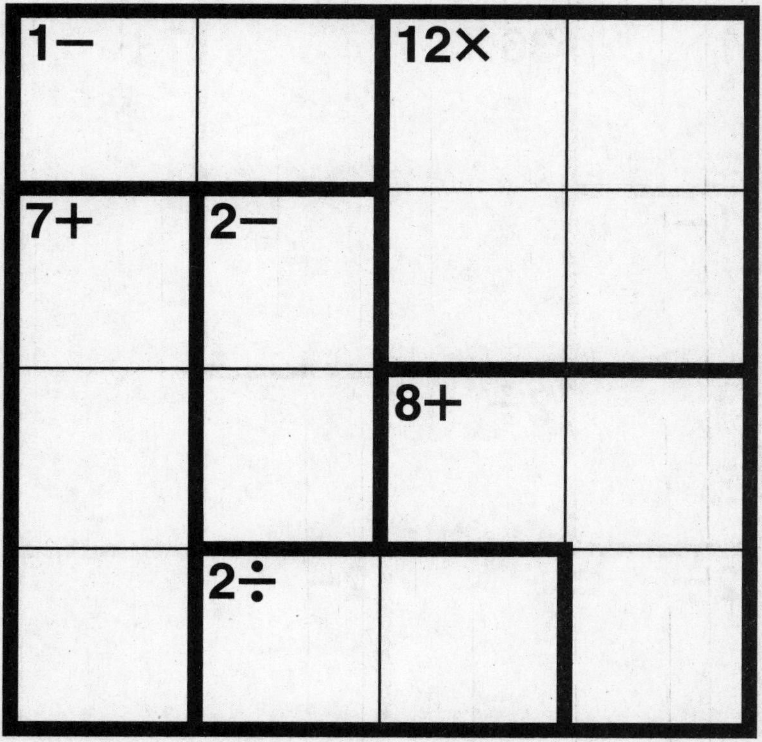

1	36×		7+
1−			
	2÷		
2÷		2−	

1−	2÷		4×
	9+		
		7+	
	1−		

130 Challenging +/−/×/÷

1−	**8×**	**1−**	
		2÷	
6+		**4**	**8+**

Challenging +/−/×/÷ 131

6×	2÷	1−	
		7+	
	9+		
1−			1

5+	1−	2÷	
		5+	24×
1−			
1−		3	

6×		2÷	
1−		1−	
	8+		
24×			1

6×		7+	1−
	4+		
2÷			1−
	1−		

Challenging +/−/×/÷ 135

1−	5+	12×	
			3−
1−		8+	
2÷			

2−		16×	
1−	5+		
	1−		
2÷		1−	

Challenging +/−/×/÷ 137

6×	3−		2
		1−	
1−		2÷	4+
2−			

138 Challenging +/−/×/÷

1−	3	8×	
	2÷		5+
7+		3	
		1−	

Challenging +/−/×/÷ 139

1	8×	1−	
		3	2÷
12+		7+	

12×		6×	
2÷		9+	
1−			2÷
	4+		

2÷		2−	
12×			9+
1−		7+	

2−	2÷	5+	
		24×	
1−			2÷
12×			

12×			2÷
9+	2÷		
	5+	1−	
		4+	

1	24×		
1−	2÷	1−	
		4+	5+
2÷			

2÷	1−		5+
	12×		
1−		5+	
	8×		

2÷	24×	2−	
			3−
7+	2−	8+	

Challenging +/−/×/÷ 147

1−		3−	
2−		24×	
5+	2÷		
	4	1−	

2÷		2−	
1−		4	6×
4	7+		
		2÷	

2÷		6×	
8+	8+		
			12×
1−			

5+		2÷	1−
1−	3		
	8×		
2÷		1−	

Easy +/−/×/÷ 151

75×		3−		2÷	3÷
3+ 1		2÷			
2	24× 4	10× 5	5− 6	1	3÷ 3
12×	4	2	8+ 3	5	1
	9+ 3	11+ 6	5	3÷ 2	9+ 4
3	4	2÷ 1	2	6	5

152 Easy +/−/×/÷

75×	3÷		4+		16×
		3÷			
3+	2÷	80×	2	5−	8+
96×	5+		10+		13+

Easy +/−/×/÷ 153

20×		**14+**		**3×**	
18×			**25×**		**96×**
3+					
	11+	**36×**		**3−**	
4		**7+**		**3÷**	
5−				**8+**	

154 Easy +/−/×/÷

3−		**3−**		**54×**	
3÷	**3÷**	**80×**		**2**	
		5−		**11+**	**20×**
8+	**3÷**		**1**		
		24×			**2×**
20×		**3−**			

1−	5−		5+	15×	
16×				5−	
2−			10+	2÷	6+
2÷		6+			
108×			10×	2÷	
	8+				4

156 Easy +/−/×/÷

48×	11+		11+		
		16×			3÷
10×		5−		2÷	
12×			20×		11+
6+	7+			192×	

24×	3÷		5+		25×
		9+			
11+			5−		36×
11+	3−		15×		
	3×	12×		12+	
		3−			

158 Easy +/−/×/÷

5+	3−	5+		11+	4
		6×	9+		11+
3−					
	80×		15×		1−
3−	2÷			4×	
		3÷			

8×		2÷		25×	2
7+		3÷	2−		
	15×			2−	
11+		5+	7+	2−	
	5−			3÷	
2		20×		2÷	

4	9×		11+	3÷	
3+		3−		3−	
	1−		10+		1−
2−		5−	1−		
	192×		2÷	75×	

Easy +/−/×/÷ 161

6+	2÷		1	2÷	
	7+		20×	30×	
3÷	20×			9×	24×
1−	6+		60×	6×	
	2−				

162 Easy +/−/×/÷

15+	2×		11+		3÷
		1−			
	11+	15+		2÷	1
9×					80×
		1−	2÷		
2÷				2÷	

3−	10×	72×	3÷		8+
				4×	
1−	2÷				2÷
	3+		10+		
5+	7+	4−	6		6×
			1−		

15+	5−		6×		8+
	10×	11+			
		1−	16×	1	15×
3+	2÷				
		2÷		60×	
3	3−		1−		

16×		75×		2÷	3÷
	3+				
1−	2−		2−		4−
	5−		2÷		
11+			2÷	6+	12×
11+		4			

6×		11+		2÷	
	1−		6+		6
10×		5−	9+	2−	
13+	5				15×
	5−	40×		3÷	
		2			

6×	2÷		3−	180×	
	10+				
24×		14+		11+	3+
3÷					
3−	12×		5−	8×	6
	8+				

168 Easy +/−/×/÷

3+		40×	45×		3÷
5+			5−		
3÷	7+			24×	2−
		5−	3−		
2−				2÷	3−
1−		1−			

4×		12+	15+		
	5−			2÷	
11+		6+	1−	1−	
	8+			2÷	
96×		2÷		10×	
			5−		

96×		3−	2÷	18×	
2−				11+	
	6+	1−	3−		2÷
5−				24×	
	7+	5−	9+		4−

Medium +/−/×/÷ 171

3+		10+	1−	2−	
2÷				15×	
		11+	4−		5+
1−	3−		2÷		
		3−	2÷	12×	
10×					4

2÷		16+		5−	
3÷				1−	2÷
1−	6+		5−		
	3−			5+	2÷
1−		16×			
3÷			15×		

Medium +/−/×/÷ 173

18×	60×			3−	3−
	48×	30×			
				9+	3÷
11+	8+				
		11+		5−	15×
	3+		3		

72×		3−		5−	
		4	1−		10+
3−		3−			
2−		2÷		30×	
6+	6×	120×			
		5−		12×	

2−	3÷		24×		4−
	20×		12×		
5−	4−			10+	1−
		14+	11+		
144×					5×
			2		

176 Medium +/−/×/÷

18×		4	16×	14+	
	3+			6+	
60×		5−	11+		9+
3÷	2−		5−		3−
	1−		1−		

Medium +/−/×/÷ 177

10×		4	1−		11+
	3÷		24×		
48×		2÷		20×	
2−		2÷			6×
	1−		5−		
2÷		4−		2−	

2−	15×		11+	5+	
	7+	1−			2÷
			2÷	1−	
30×		5−			6+
3÷			7+	120×	
	3÷				

80×			9×	10+	
	50×			72×	
		5−			
2÷		3−		3−	
1−	144×		3+		2−
			1−		

180 Medium +/−/×/÷

3+		720×			8+
4−	1−	48×			
		2−		7+	
2÷	1−		4×		13+
				9×	
48×					

Medium +/−/×/÷ 181

18×	3÷		10×	1−	
	2÷	9+		5−	
			3÷		13+
40×	1−	1−	3÷		
			1−	10×	
	6×				

8×	2÷	4−		2−	4
		14+	3+		48×
3÷		11+	2÷	7+	
1−				7+	
3÷			4	2−	

Medium +/−/×/÷ 183

10+		36×		1−	
2×		1−	5+		
	9+		6	24×	
90×		3÷			
14+	12×		5−		
			6+		

184 Medium +/−/×/÷

11+	108×		2÷		6+
			14+		
2÷	1−			6+	1−
		3+			
2÷	4×	2−		90×	3÷

Medium +/−/×/÷

1−		3÷		12×	13+
3+	15×				
	5−	1−	2−	6×	
144×					3+
	3÷		80×		
		5−			5

186 Medium +/−/×/÷

8+		2÷	2÷	60×	
	18+			3×	
		1−	6+		
	9×			12+	4
2−					3÷
	3−		10×		

Medium +/−/×/÷ 187

2÷		96×	6×		6+
3÷				5	
	3+		60×		
3−	16+		1	3÷	
			1−		10+
15×			3÷		

11+		1	120×	1−	
2÷	1−			2÷	
	17+			4−	
2÷			3÷	3	15+
	2÷				
15×			48×		

1−	15+	3÷		4×	
			9×	1−	
10×					1−
3−		11+		2	
3−	6+			14+	
	4	3−			

190 Medium +/−/×/÷

15×	10+		2÷		3÷
	1−		2−		
12×		2÷		11+	
5−		3−	3÷		120×
	8+			2÷	
		4−			

13+		3−		13+	
	24×				
7+		24×	1−		3÷
	25×		5−		
8+			4	120×	
		2÷			

14+		2−	2÷		6
			2−	15+	
11+					1−
72×	2÷		9+	3×	
	2÷	20×			
			13+		

Medium +/−/×/÷   193

90×		10+		24×	1−
2−		7+			
					3÷
3+	72×		100×		
	11+		9×		14+

194 Medium +/−/×/÷

4	12×	11+		5+	
		1−		3÷	1−
3−	4×		1−		
	5			1−	5−
60×		1−			
		5−		2÷	

2−		5+		4−	
5×		2÷	2−	11+	
3÷					1−
	16+				
2−		4−	16+		2
1−				5+	

3−	2−		3÷		6×
	1−		5−		
4−		6+	1−	11+	
24×	3				11+
		1−	20×		
3÷				30×	

Medium +/−/×/÷ 197

80×			3÷		1−
	11+		270×		
5		1−			
2÷		2−		2−	
54×	13+		8×		20×

198 Medium +/−/×/÷

3÷	3+		1−		11+
	6+		120×		
2÷			3÷		5+
3−		15+		9×	
1−					1−
	2−		1−		

Medium +/−/×/÷ 199

12+		20×	3−	54×	
				1	
11+		1−	2÷	25×	
	1−			2−	
15×		20×			2÷
	2÷		1−		

11+		18×	2÷		4−
3−	2÷			15+	
		6+			
1−	4−	2−		8×	
		21+			12×
			3−		

3−		3−		2÷	
2÷	60×	2−		5−	
			3−		4−
3+	48×		3÷		
		3−		1−	
2−		5−		2−	

2÷	15+		5+		1−
		10×	3÷		
4−				24×	
2÷		36×		2−	
12×			120×	8+	
	1−				

Medium +/−/×/÷ 203

3−		2	3−	3÷	4−
1−	1−				
	3+	6×		15×	
6×		1−		3−	
	6×		20×		2÷
1−		1−			

204 Medium +/−/×/÷

5−	1−	10+		1−	2÷
		5×			
12+				18×	
5+		12×	3÷		6+
	11+			24×	
		10+			

Medium +/−/×/÷ 205

2−	3−		16+	5−	
	36×			40×	3
			3÷		
7+		5×		1−	1−
1−					
	24×		6+		

11+		7+		240×	
	5−	1−	2÷	1−	
6					
10+	2−		3600×	2	3×
		36×			

Medium +/−/×/÷ 207

6×		5−	15×	3−	
1−				3÷	
1−	2÷		3+	2−	5−
	7+				
7+		8+	10+	1−	
3				1−	

3	144×			2−	2÷
1−		3+			
	3÷	10×		1−	
2÷		24×		6+	
	14+	1−		12×	
			11+		

7+		3	4−		12+
	75×	1−			
		4×		2−	
2÷		20×		1−	
5−	2−			6+	
		14+			

2÷	1−		3÷		10+
	9+		7+		
5		288×			
3−				5−	
4×		8+		48×	
	16+				

Medium +/−/×/÷ 211

9+		10×		24×	1
	1−	24×			1−
1−				3÷	
	1−	2−	2		9+
6×			2÷	3−	
		4			

6×	72×		2−	11+	
					11+
2÷		4×		11+	
80×	5				
		17+		108×	

Medium +/−/×/÷ 213

1−		**1−**		**5−**	
1−	**1**	**2÷**		**8×**	
	9+		**1−**	**3÷**	
2÷	**3÷**				**20+**
	13+				
10+		**2÷**			

214 Medium +/−/×/÷

1−	17+	3−		5−	
			1−		20×
2−			4×	1−	
3−					3−
2÷	20×		1−		
		2÷		2÷	

15+		2÷		2×	
12+			20×		11+
	19+				
					15+
1−	2×		240×		
		6			

216 Medium +/−/×/÷

5−	11+		90×		3÷
		2÷			
17+		13+	3×	2−	
					120×
	6×		60×		
		1−			

Medium +/−/×/÷ 217

1−		12×		2÷	
2÷	8+		5−		1−
	144×	1−		12×	
		2÷	20×		
	3÷			1−	1−
1		3÷			

2÷	30×		3÷		1−
	11+		5−		
3	3−		8+	2−	30×
30×		6×			
			2−		5+
	3−		3−		

Medium +/−/×/÷ 219

12+	1−	2÷	1−	2−	6
					3÷
	10×		3−		
3	5−	2÷		3÷	15+
25×		2÷	3÷		

1−	180×		6+		
		3÷		10+	
5−	1−	9+			2−
			5	20+	
1−	13+	2−			

Medium +/−/×/÷ 221

6+		**8+**		**15+**	
2÷	**1−**				
	1−	**3÷**		**25×**	
30×		**12×**			
	5−		**20×**	**72×**	
1−					

2	7+	30×		11+	10+
1−					
	15+		2×		
18+	30×			144×	2÷
				10×	

Medium +/−/×/÷ 223

3×		11+			15+
	72×		2÷		
3÷	2−			5−	6×
		15+	12×		
40×				18+	

2×		9+	15+	1−	
3÷				10+	
	2−			3÷	
72×		12+	6+		40×
1−				4−	

Medium +/−/×/÷ 225

3÷	1−	2−		4×	
		2−	2÷		12+
3−					
11+		6+	2−	1−	
2−	1−			432×	
		2÷			

226 Medium +/−/×/÷

8×	3÷		2−		120×
		8+			
24×		4−		18+	2
10+		2−			
	20×		48×		
	6+				

Medium +/−/×/÷ 227

13+	20×		1−	5−	
	1−			3÷	3
	1−	1−			3−
12×		5−		1−	
	2÷		2÷		30×
	1−				

2−	8×			120×	5+
	5−		2÷		
4−	2÷	4−			
			2÷	2÷	15+
7+	2−				
		1−			

Medium +/−/×/÷ 229

864×			8+	2−	1−
1−	1−		2−	2÷	3÷
	4−				
6+	16×	8+		30×	4−

4−		**1−**	**2÷**	**12+**	
12×	**2**				**3−**
	13+	**2−**	**1−**	**6+**	
					19+
60×		**4−**			
		5+			

24×		14+			1−
	1−		3−		
6×		1−	2−	1−	
1−				10+	
20×	2−		2÷		3−
		3−		3	

232 Challenging +/−/×/÷

5+	1−		1−		12×
	5	12×			
3÷	3÷		6×	9+	6+
	2−				
2−	2÷		3÷		3÷
	1−		3−		

Challenging +/−/×/÷ 233

1−	2−	8+	10+	1−	
				24×	
2−	5+			4×	
	11+				10+
2−	1−	2÷	1−	9+	

18+		5	3÷	9×	
	4×				10+
		2÷	4		
17+			120×		
			8+	24×	
	1−				

3−	10×		1−		30×
	11+	2−	2÷	11+	
2−		5−		2−	
2−	11+		9+		1−
		11+			

360×	1−		3÷		13+
	9+		10×		
3−	2÷		24×		2−
	5−		1−		
3−		1−		1−	

Challenging +/−/×/÷ 237

6×		2−		2÷	
1−	3÷		6+		2−
	3−		2−		
3÷		12×	40×	1−	
1−				1−	
2−				6×	

12×			3÷	1−	10+
60×		2−			
	1−		2÷	5−	15×
7+		5−			
			1−	1−	1−
60×					

Challenging +/−/×/÷ 239

2−	3÷	5+		3÷	2−
		10×	15+		
2÷				3−	
2÷	7+			7+	5+
		2÷	1−		
1−				5−	

3−		36×		8+	
3÷	1−		1−		
		1−		2÷	1−
1−	2−	4−			
		32×	1−		10+
7+					

Challenging +/−/×/÷ 241

2−		9×		11+	48×
6+	90×				
			2÷		
1−	24×		2−		9+
		13+	11+		
2÷					

242 Challenging +/−/×/÷

14+	9×		12×		12+
720×			16+		
	8+		12+	10+	
2÷					1−
		3÷			

2÷	13+	60×			
		24×	4−	3÷	
2÷				1−	3−
	8+		2÷		
4−				5−	
		15+			

15+			9+	36×	
1−					3÷
	3÷	3−	1−	1−	
6×					7+
	7+		30×		
2−		1−		2÷	

Challenging +/−/×/÷ 245

144×		2−		17+	
	2−				2÷
3÷		80×	144×		
					2−
10×		3	90×		
		2−			

2÷	4−	2÷		2−	10+
		16×	11+		
4−					3−
	5+		48×		
15+		11+	1−		3×

Challenging +/−/×/÷ 247

2−		1−	8+		
11+			11+		
3		3÷		2−	
15+			5×	1−	
		3÷			240×
1−					

13+			25×		1−
12×	3÷	12+			
			1−	1−	
11+		12×		2−	
1				9+	1−
15×					

3÷		10+		72×	20×
16+					
		1−		3−	
11+		5−		1−	
	6	14+	6+		3−
1−					

4−	2÷	7+		60×	7+
5+		4−		2−	
36×	9+		30×		1−
		25×	288×		

Challenging +/−/×/÷ 251

1−	3−	9+			7+
		7+	17+		
20+					2÷
		2−	4×		
3÷				45×	
		30×			

72×		10+		1−	
2−			1−		1440×
	4−		1−		
5−	1−		3÷		
	4−	13+	2−		
2					

3÷		150×	1−	9+	2−
2−		2−			
3÷		3−		270×	
2	9+		1−		6+
3−					

3−		2−	10×	19+	
2−					
1−	2−	2÷			
		13+		4−	
5−			60×		12×
24×					

2−	7+		10+		36×
		4−			
14+	7+		4−		
		9+		3÷	
3−	7+		36×		1−
		2−			

400×			3÷		11+
	3−		3−		
	8+		7+		
13+				80×	
1−		3−			6+
	7+		2÷		

24×	4−		1−		10+
	2÷		4−		
	2−	5−	10+	3−	
2−					3−
	6+			16+	
40×					

12+		60×		2÷	
				13+	4−
12×		6	1−		
5	2÷				5+
60×		4×			
			120×		

11+		2÷		5×	
		6+	1−		19+
12+					
	1−	3÷	2÷	1−	
6×					24×
		1−			

576×		13+			9+
13+		7+	10+	1−	
3				2÷	
16+	6+			11+	
			1−		4

Challenging +/−/×/÷ 261

36×		9+		1	13+
120×		11+			
			3÷	5−	
12+				2÷	
	4+		19+		
		2−			

12×			13+		
4	3÷		4−		9+
17+		1−	1−		
8+					24×
	18×	1−		2÷	

30×		6×	2÷	16+	30×
1−					
7+	2÷				
	15×		14+		11+
10×		12×	2−		
2−			1		

2÷		15×		5−	
8+	7+		2−		11+
		2÷			
2−	36×		30×		2−
		6+	7+		
24×				2÷	

6×	3÷		18+		
	9+	16+			3−
2−			3÷		
			3−		2−
8+	2		10×		
	1−			5−	

15+			48×		
9×				120×	
30×		4−	3÷		2−
	2÷			3÷	
24×		1−	2−		8+

Challenging +/−/×/÷   267

6×		30×	8+		2−
	1−		3−		
5−			3÷	17+	
	1−	24×			
120×			5−		2÷
			1−		

30×			15+		1−
48×	1	5−			
				180×	
5+		6×	288×		
90×					2÷
	10+				

1−		4−		13+	
60×	4×		1−		
			2÷	2÷	
12×		13+		2−	
			24×		6+
3÷		15×			

10+		2÷		5×	
	60×	1−		6	
4−		5+		6×	12×
		1−	5−		
13+				240×	
		3−			

5+		1−	2−	3−	
2−				6×	
60×	10+		2−		12+
		5+	3−		
2÷				2÷	
3	1−		8×		

1−		3−	3−	5+	
60×				18+	
	3−		5+		
1	2÷		2÷		
5−		3−	1−	3−	
1−				1−	

Challenging +/−/×/÷ 273

8×	17+		11+		
				2÷	
	2÷	1−		1	12+
90×		2−			
	24×		21+	2÷	

2÷		3−		5+	
480×	2−		6+		2÷
		2÷		180×	
5×		36×	48×	13+	

12×		7+		4−	
13+				300×	
	2÷				2÷
30×	15×		10+		
	2÷		72×		
3−				7+	

24×	2−		2−		9+
	48×			1	
	9+	2÷		12+	
		2÷	4−		
1−	6+			2÷	3÷
		1−			

Challenging +/−/×/÷ 277

1−	2−	40×	6	3−	
				144×	
6+					5
12+			30×	13+	
9+	7+				
		1−		2÷	

5−		60×			11+
3÷	3÷		3−		
	3−	2−		1−	
8+		4−			10+
	3÷		3−		
1−		11+			

Challenging +/−/×/÷ 279

1−	24×		11+		10×
		14+			
2−			2	4−	2−
2÷		720×			
1−	6+				2−
		3	2÷		

75×	5+		3÷		6+
		30×	3−		
12×				1−	
	12+	2−		120×	
		6×			
1−		1−		1−	

Challenging +/−/×/÷ 281

10×			11+	2−	2÷
3−					
3−			90×		
1−		360×	9+		
3÷				1−	4−
2	2−				

6+		11+	2÷	1−	12×
2÷					
	2÷		14+		
2÷		240×	3÷		5
			5−	2÷	1−
2−					

Challenging +/−/×/÷ 283

30×		9+	2÷		7+
			2−		
2÷	7+			9+	
	15×		2÷	4−	
48×	60×			9+	
			6×		

284 Challenging +/−/×/÷

1−	4−		20×		3÷
	14+	6×		13+	
		2÷			
15+	2−		2÷		6
		3−		7+	
	3−		2÷		

Challenging +/−/×/÷ 285

90×		3−		4−	
		60×	10+		
2÷	3−			120×	3
		14+			
720×			6×		
		3÷		2÷	

10+	3−		6×		12+
		2÷			
30×		1−		5+	
1−		1−		2÷	
2÷	10+		2−		3−
	3÷		2−		

1−		3÷		4−	
5+	10×		72×		2−
	10+			13+	
		10+			
180×			2	9+	
		30×			

3÷		60×	3÷	10+	
1−					5−
5	15×		14+		
		8+			2−
2÷			1−	24×	
2−					

Challenging +/−/×/÷ 289

5−		7+	2−	2÷	
12×				1−	
4−	16+		30×		10+
1−	4−		2−		3−
	3−		5+		

290 Challenging +/−/×/÷

36×			2−		13+
12+		6			
		10×			1−
11+		24×			
	15+		3−	18×	
2÷					

Challenging +/−/×/÷ 291

2÷	72×		11+		3−
	1−			2−	
2−		1−	2−		6×
	10×			9+	
8+		3−			1−
		10+			

1−		18×		5+	
15+	2÷			3−	1−
		3−			
10×		1−		2−	3÷
	3−		10+		
2÷				6×	

Challenging +/−/×/÷ 293

2÷	2÷	1	10+	240×	
				3−	
20×		2÷			
360×		2−		5+	4−
2÷		16+			
				3−	

3÷		2÷	16+		
1−	24×			10×	
		3÷			3−
6+	15×		72×		
		11+	9+		2−
1−					

48×		4−	1−	6+	
9+					48×
		10+	15+		
5+					4−
	2÷		2÷		
4−		5+		2−	

12×	3÷		2−	10+	
		3−			9+
1−			2÷		
2÷		2−		10+	
7+			8+	36×	
	7+				

4−		2÷		24×	
2÷	1−	2÷	2÷		
				1−	7+
5+	1−	2−	4−		
				14+	
2÷		2−			

14+		2−	24×	1−	
					10+
2−	2÷	3−			
		12+		14+	
3	12×	3÷			
			15+		

40×			10+		
16+		2−		9+	
		4−	2÷	6	
24×				12+	
	12+				
6	2÷		12+		

14+	1−		2−		18×
		11+		6×	
9+					
3÷		360×	10×		11+
12+					
	3÷			6	

ANSWERS

1

7+ 4	3+ 1	6× 3	2
3	2	3− 4	1
5+ 2	3	1 1	12× 4
1 1	2÷ 4	2	3

2

4+ 3	1	3− 4	2 2
2÷ 2	4	1	12× 3
3− 1	6× 3	2	4
4	2 2	4+ 3	1

3

12× 3	4	3+ 1	2÷ 2
4+ 1	3	2	4
2− 4	2 2	4+ 3	1
2	3− 1	4	3 3

4

6× 3	2÷ 4	2	1 1
2	3 3	3− 1	4
3− 1	2÷ 2	7+ 4	3
4	1	6× 3	2

5

7+ 4	3	2÷ 2	1
2 2	3− 4	1	6× 3
2− 3	1	4 4	2
3+ 1	2	7+ 3	4

6

6× 2	3− 1	12× 3	4
3	4	2 2	3+ 1
3− 1	1− 3	4	2
4	2÷ 2	1	3 3

7

5+ 1	2÷ 4	18× 2	3
4	2	3	3− 1
5+ 2	4+ 3	3− 1	4
3	1	4	2 2

8

2÷ 2	1	10+ 3	4
3− 1	9+ 2	4	3
4	3	4× 1	2
12× 3	4	2	1 1

9

7+ 3	4	3− 1	2÷ 2
1− 2	3	4	1
3− 4	2÷ 1	2 2	36× 3
1	2	3	4

10

18× 3	2	3− 4	3+ 1
3− 4	3	1	2
1	2÷ 4	2	1− 3
2÷ 2	1	3 3	4

11

7+ 4	2 2	2− 1	3
2	9× 1	3	2÷ 4
1	3	8× 4	2
7+ 3	4	2	1

12

3+ 1	2	7+ 3	4 4
2 2	3× 1	4	6× 3
1− 4	3	1	2
3	2÷ 4	2	1

13

2÷ 2	12× 3	4	2− 1
4	3+ 2	1	3
3× 1	4	1− 3	2÷ 2
3	1	2	4

14

2− 3	7+ 4	1− 2	1
1	3	2÷ 4	2
2÷ 4	3+ 2	1	36× 3
2	1 1	3	4

15

2÷ 2	7+ 4	6× 1	3
4	3	2	3− 1
1 1	6× 2	3	4
4+ 3	1	2÷ 4	2

16

4 4	7+ 3	2÷ 2	1
6× 1	4	24× 3	2
3	3+ 2	1	4
2	3− 1	4	3 3

17

4+ 3	6× 2	3− 1	4
1	3	2÷ 4	5+ 2
3− 4	1	2	3
24× 2	4	3	1 1

18

5+ 1	8+ 4	2	9× 3
4	2	3	1
6× 2	3	3− 1	4
2− 3	1	2÷ 4	2

19

2− **2**	4+ **3**	**1**	4 **4**
4	3+ **1**	7+ **3**	6× **2**
8+ **1**	**2**	**4**	**3**
3	**4**	2÷ **2**	**1**

20

2− **2**	**4**	2− **3**	**1**
3+ **1**	**2**	12× **4**	**3**
36× **4**	**3**	**1**	2÷ **2**
3	3+ **1**	**2**	**4**

21

2÷ **1**	**2**	1− **4**	**3**
7+ **3**	**1**	2÷ **2**	**4**
2÷ **4**	**3**	3× **1**	2 **2**
2	4 **4**	**3**	**1**

22

1− **1**	**2**	7+ **4**	1− **3**
2÷ **4**	4+ **1**	**3**	**2**
2	**3**	8× **1**	**4**
12× **3**	**4**	**2**	**1**

23

2− **4**	**2**	8+ **3**	1− **1**
2÷ **1**	12× **3**	**4**	**2**
2	**4**	**1**	7+ **3**
3 **3**	3+ **1**	**2**	**4**

24

3− **4**	3+ **1**	**2**	1− **3**
1	2÷ **2**	2− **3**	**4**
18× **3**	**4**	**1**	1− **2**
2	**3**	4 **4**	**1**

25

2 ²	**3** ^{9×}	**1** ^{3−}	**4**
3	**1**	**4** ^{24×}	**2**
1 ⁷⁺	**4** ^{2÷}	**2**	**3**
4	**2**	**3** ^{2−}	**1**

26

4 ^{16×}	**1**	**3** ⁷⁺	**2**
3 ³	**4**	**2**	**1** ⁵⁺
2 ^{1−}	**3**	**1** ^{3−}	**4**
1 ^{2÷}	**2**	**4**	**3** ³

27

2 ^{1−}	**3**	**4** ^{2÷}	**1** ⁵⁺
3 ^{2−}	**1**	**2**	**4**
4 ⁵⁺	**2** ^{2÷}	**1** ¹	**3** ^{18×}
1	**4**	**3**	**2**

28

1 ¹	**3** ⁹⁺	**2**	**4**
3 ^{1−}	**4**	**1** ^{3−}	**2** ²
2 ^{2÷}	**1**	**4**	**3** ^{9×}
4 ^{2÷}	**2**	**3**	**1**

29

3 ^{12×}	**4** ^{2÷}	**2**	**1** ^{1−}
4	**1** ⁴⁺	**3**	**2**
2 ^{6×}	**3**	**1** ^{3−}	**4**
1	**2** ²	**4** ^{12×}	**3**

30

2 ⁸⁺	**4** ⁸⁺	**1**	**3**
4	**2**	**3** ^{1−}	**1** ¹
1 ¹	**3** ^{9×}	**2**	**4** ^{2÷}
3	**1**	**4** ⁴	**2**

31

³⁺2	³⁻1	¹⁻4	³3
1	4	3	²÷2
¹⁻3	⁵⁺2	²ˣ1	4
4	3	2	1

32

⁴⁺3	1	²÷2	⁴4
²÷4	¹⁻3	1	¹⁻2
2	4	³⁶ˣ3	1
²÷1	2	4	3

33

¹⁻2	3	⁴ˣ4	1
²÷4	2	1	¹¹⁺3
⁴⁺3	³⁻1	2	4
1	4	³3	2

34

³⁻1	²÷4	2	³3
4	⁶ˣ2	3	⁸ˣ1
²⁻3	1	³⁻4	2
⁵⁺2	3	1	4

35

¹⁻2	3	¹¹⁺4	1
³3	²÷1	2	4
⁵⁺1	²÷4	⁹ˣ3	2
4	2	1	3

36

³⁻1	²÷4	2	⁶⁺3
4	¹⁻2	3	1
¹⁸ˣ3	³⁻1	4	2
2	3	⁵⁺1	4

37

2÷ 4	2	2− 1	3
1− 2	12× 4	3	2÷ 1
3	3− 1	4	2
4+ 1	3	2÷ 2	4

38

8× 4	2÷ 1	2	10+ 3
1	2	3	4
18× 3	3− 4	1	7+ 2
2	3	4	1

39

7+ 3	3− 1	4	4× 2
4	1− 3	2	1
2÷ 1	2	1− 3	4
2	4 4	2− 1	3

40

6+ 1	1− 3	4	2 2
3	8+ 1	2	4
2	2÷ 4	1	9× 3
4 4	2	3	1

41

1− 3	4	4+ 1	2÷ 2
4× 1	2	3	4
2	9+ 3	4	2− 1
3− 4	1	2	3

42

2− 4	6+ 1	6× 3	2
2	4	1	3 3
2− 3	2÷ 2	4	5+ 1
1	1− 3	2	4

43

12× 3	4	1	2÷ 2
2÷ 2	1	10+ 3	4
1	1− 2	4	3
4	3	1− 2	1

44

2÷ 2	4	6× 3	1
3− 4	6+ 3	1	2
1	2	13+ 4	3
2− 3	1	2	4

45

9+ 3	2	3− 4	1
1− 1	4	1− 2	3
2	9× 3	1	2÷ 4
5+ 4	1	3	2

46

1− 1	4	1− 3	2
2	8+ 3	16× 1	4
3	2	4	4+ 1
4	2÷ 1	2	3

47

2÷ 4	3× 1	3	2 2
2	4 4	1	1− 3
2− 1	1− 3	7+ 2	4
3	2	4	1

48

3− 4	72× 3	2÷ 2	1
1	2	4	3
1− 3	8+ 4	1	2÷ 2
2	1 1	3	4

49

2÷ 4	2	10+ 3	1− 1
12× 1	3	4	2
3	1	2− 2	4
2 2	4	2− 1	3

50

2− 3	4× 2	1	1− 4
1	1− 4	2	3
2÷ 2	3	7+ 4	2÷ 1
4	1 1	3	2

51

5+ 1	4	6× 2	2− 3
2÷ 4	1− 2	3	1
2	3	8× 1	4
4+ 3	1	4 4	2

52

3− 4	1 1	1− 3	1− 2
1	2÷ 2	4	3
8+ 3	4	2 2	4× 1
2	3	1	4

53

6× 1	2÷ 4	5+ 3	2
3	2	16× 1	4
2	3 3	4	2− 1
8× 4	1	2	3

54

3− 4	2÷ 1	2	1− 3
1	12× 3	4	2
5+ 3	2− 2	6+ 1	4
2	4	3 3	1

55

12× 1	3	2÷ 4	2
4	2× 1	2	8+ 3
1− 3	2÷ 2	1	4
2	4	3 3	1

56

2÷ 4	6× 1	3	2
2	3 3	5+ 1	4
1− 3	2	32× 4	2− 1
1	4	2	3

57

6× 3	2	4+ 1	48× 4
2÷ 4	1	2	3
2	8+ 3	4	1
1	4	1− 3	2

58

2÷ 2	1	10+ 3	4
12× 1	6+ 2	4 4	3
4	3	1	2÷ 2
3	2− 4	2	1

59

6+ 3	16× 4	1	2 2
2	2− 1	4	1− 3
1	3	6× 2	4
2÷ 4	2	3	1

60

2÷ 2	4	9× 3	1
1 1	1− 2	3− 4	3
1− 4	3	1	8+ 2
3	1 1	2	4

61

24× 2	2− 3	1	5+ 4
3	4	1− 2	1
3− 4	1	3	1− 2
1 1	2÷ 2	4	3

62

2− 3	1	24× 2	3− 4
7+ 2	3	4	1
1	4	1− 3	2
2÷ 4	2	4+ 1	3

63

1− 3	2÷ 1	2 2	3− 4
4	2	9+ 3	1
6× 1	3	4	2
2	3− 4	1	3 3

64

12× 3	2÷ 2	1	4 4
4	3 3	5+ 2	1− 1
1	7+ 4	3	2
2	1	7+ 4	3

65

6× 1	3	2÷ 4	2
3 3	2	6+ 1	8+ 4
3− 4	1	2	3
2÷ 2	4	3	1

66

2÷ 2	12× 3	1	4
4	1− 2	3	2− 1
5+ 1	2− 4	2	3
3	1	2÷ 4	2

67

3− 1	1− 3	4	9+ 2
4	2÷ 1	2	3
12× 2	4 4	3	1
3	2	3− 1	4

68

6× 3	2	1	24× 4
3− 4	1	2÷ 2	3
7+ 1	3 3	4	2
2	4	4+ 3	1

69

12× 4	1	9+ 3	2
2÷ 2	3	3− 1	4
1	2÷ 2	4	6× 3
3 3	4	2	1

70

2÷ 1	6× 2	3	1− 4
2	2− 1	2÷ 4	3
12+ 4	3	2	2÷ 1
3	4	1	2

71

2÷ 2	1	10+ 4	3
8+ 1	4	3	8× 2
3	4× 2	1	4
1− 4	3	2	1

72

1− 4	2− 3	1	10+ 2
3	2÷ 2	4	1
2÷ 2	1	6× 3	4
3− 1	4	2	3

73

¹⁻ 2	3	²÷ 1	³⁻ 4
⁴⁸× 3	4	2	1
4	⁴⁺ 1	3	¹⁻ 2
1	²⁻ 2	4	3

74

²⁻ 3	1	⁶⁺ 2	³⁻ 4
²÷ 2	4	3	1
⁷⁺ 4	³ 3	1	²⁴× 2
1	2	4	3

75

²÷ 2	⁶× 3	⁸⁺ 4	1
4	2	¹ 1	3
⁶⁺ 3	1	2	²⁴× 4
³⁻ 1	4	3	2

76

² 2	⁵⁺ 1	²÷ 4	⁶⁺ 3
¹²× 3	4	2	1
4	⁴⁺ 3	1	2
1	¹⁻ 2	3	⁴ 4

77

³⁻ 1	²⁴× 3	4	2
4	² 2	⁹⁺ 1	3
²÷ 2	1	3	³⁻ 4
¹⁻ 3	4	2	1

78

²⁴× 3	2	⁴ 4	⁶⁺ 1
4	²⁻ 1	3	2
²÷ 2	⁸⁺ 4	1	3
1	3	²÷ 2	4

79

3− **1**	**4**	12× **3**	6+ **2**
2÷ **2**	**1**	**4**	**3**
4	12× **3**	**2**	**1**
3 **3**	**2**	5+ **1**	**4**

80

6+ **1**	1− **3**	**2**	8× **4**
3	16× **4**	**1**	**2**
2	**1**	**4**	2− **3**
2÷ **4**	**2**	3 **3**	**1**

81

1− **4**	**3**	8× **1**	2 **2**
2− **3**	**4**	**2**	3− **1**
1	12+ **2**	**3**	**4**
2÷ **2**	**1**	**4**	**3**

82

2÷ **2**	**1**	1− **3**	**4**
8+ **1**	7+ **2**	**4**	6× **3**
3	4 **4**	**1**	**2**
4	1− **3**	**2**	1 **1**

83

12× **1**	11+ **3**	**4**	**2**
4	1− **1**	**2**	3 **3**
3	**2**	2− **1**	3− **4**
2÷ **2**	**4**	**3**	**1**

84

2÷ **1**	1− **2**	**3**	3− **4**
2	3 **3**	7+ **4**	**1**
4 **4**	12× **1**	**2**	1− **3**
3	**4**	**1**	**2**

85

1− 3	8× 2	4	1
2	4 4	2− 1	3
8+ 1	3	2÷ 2	4
4	2− 1	3	2 2

86

2÷ 1	2	4 4	12× 3
1− 2	3	1	4
1− 4	5+ 1	7+ 3	2
3	4	2	1 1

87

2 2	12× 4	3	1
1− 1	2	2÷ 4	7+ 3
4+ 3	1	2	4
1− 4	3	1− 1	2

88

5+ 4	1	24× 3	2
2 2	2− 3	1	4
8+ 3	4	2÷ 2	1
1	2 2	1− 4	3

89

2 2	12× 4	3	1
5+ 4	1	2÷ 2	3 3
2− 1	3	4	8× 2
1− 3	2	1	4

90

6+ 3	8× 1	2	4 4
2	4	4+ 3	1
1	9+ 2	1− 4	3
4	3	2÷ 1	2

91

8+ 3	**4** 4	**1−** 2	1
1	**24×** 3	4	2
4	**2÷** 2	1	**1−** 3
2÷ 2	1	**3** 3	4

92

24× 2	**2÷** 1	**12×** 4	3
3	2	**5+** 1	4
4	**5+** 3	2	**1−** 1
1 1	**1−** 4	3	2

93

3− 1	4	**3** 3	**1−** 2
24× 2	**3−** 1	4	3
4	3	**2÷** 2	**5+** 1
1− 3	2	1	4

94

12× 4	3	1	**6+** 2
1− 3	2	**10+** 4	1
1 1	4	2	3
2÷ 2	1	**1−** 3	4

95

8× 4	**6+** 3	2	1
1	**2÷** 2	**8+** 3	**4** 4
2	4	1	**1−** 3
2− 3	1	4	2

96

1− 4	**5+** 1	**6×** 3	2
3	4	**2÷** 2	1
6× 2	3	1	**4** 4
2÷ 1	2	**1−** 4	3

97

36× 3	4	**1−** 2	1
2÷ 1	3	**8+** 4	**9+** 2
2	1	3	4
8× 4	2	1	3

98

1− 3	4	**2÷** 2	1
2− 4	2	**1** 1	**24×** 3
2÷ 1	**4+** 3	4	2
2	1	**1−** 3	4

99

2÷ 2	1	**1−** 4	3
2− 3	**2** 2	**7+** 1	4
1	**24×** 4	**3** 3	2
4 4	3	2	1

100

5+ 1	**72×** 3	**2÷** 4	2
4	2	3	**1** 1
1− 2	4	**12×** 1	3
3	**1−** 1	2	4

101

5+ 1	4	**1−** 3	2
2÷ 2	1	**4** 4	**12×** 3
12× 3	**1−** 2	1	4
4	3	**1−** 2	1

102

2÷ 1	2	**8×** 4	**3** 3
3 3	1	2	**7+** 4
1− 4	3	1	2
2− 2	4	**2−** 3	1

103

1− **3**	**2**	5+ **1**	**4**
1− **4**	**3**	1− **2**	2÷ **1**
2× **1**	4 **4**	**3**	**2**
2	**1**	1− **4**	**3**

104

2− **3**	**1**	8× **2**	**4**
7+ **2**	1− **3**	**4**	**1**
4	2÷ **2**	6+ **1**	**3**
1	**4**	3 **3**	**2**

105

2÷ **2**	48× **4**	**3**	**1**
1	1− **2**	**4**	3 **3**
8+ **4**	**3**	1− **1**	2− **2**
3	**1**	**2**	**4**

106

12× **3**	**4**	1− **2**	**1**
2÷ **2**	**1**	1− **3**	2÷ **4**
1	1− **3**	**4**	**2**
4 **4**	**2**	4+ **1**	**3**

107

3− **4**	**1**	18× **3**	**2**
2÷ **2**	**4**	2÷ **1**	**3**
2− **1**	9+ **3**	**2**	5+ **4**
3	**2**	**4**	**1**

108

4× **4**	**1**	3 **3**	1− **2**
1	2÷ **2**	**4**	**3**
12+ **3**	**4**	2÷ **2**	**1**
2	**3**	3− **1**	**4**

109

12× 3	4	1− 2	1
1	3 3	9+ 4	2
2÷ 4	1− 2	1 1	3
2	1	1− 3	4

110

24× 2	3	4	5+ 1
4+ 3	1	1− 2	4
9+ 1	4	3	1− 2
4	2÷ 2	1	3

111

4× 4	1	9+ 2	3 3
1	24× 2	3	4
1− 2	3	4	2÷ 1
3	3− 4	1	2

112

8+ 4	2− 1	3	8× 2
3	2÷ 2	4	1
1	4	6+ 2	3
1− 2	3	1	4 4

113

1− 3	16× 4	2÷ 1	2
2	1	4	1− 3
8+ 1	3	8+ 2	4
4	2	3	1

114

1 1	6× 3	2	2÷ 4
1− 3	9+ 4	1	2
4	2	1− 3	2− 1
2	1	4	3

115

8× **1**	**2**	1− **4**	**3**
4	4+ **1**	**3**	2÷ **2**
1− **2**	**3**	2÷ **1**	**4**
1− **3**	**4**	**2**	1 **1**

116

1− **3**	**2**	2− **1**	8× **4**
12× **1**	**4**	**3**	**2**
4 **4**	**3**	9+ **2**	**1**
2÷ **2**	**1**	**4**	**3**

117

1− **1**	**2**	1− **4**	**3**
1− **2**	**3**	2÷ **1**	3− **4**
12× **3**	**4**	**2**	**1**
4 **4**	**1**	5+ **3**	**2**

118

1− **2**	**1**	1− **3**	**4**
8+ **3**	**2**	8× **4**	**1**
16× **4**	**3**	2÷ **1**	**2**
1	**4**	**2**	3 **3**

119

1− **3**	**4**	8× **1**	**2**
9+ **1**	**2**	**3**	**4**
2÷ **4**	**3**	2 **2**	9+ **1**
2	**1**	**4**	**3**

120

1− **2**	4+ **1**	**3**	3− **4**
3	2÷ **4**	**2**	**1**
2÷ **1**	**2**	24× **4**	**3**
1− **4**	**3**	**1**	**2**

121

4+ 1	3	2÷ 4	2
2÷ 2	1	2− 3	12× 4
1− 4	2− 2	1	3
3	4	2 2	1

122

3− 1	2÷ 4	2	2− 3
4	1− 2	3	1
6× 2	2− 3	5+ 1	4
3	1	2÷ 4	2

123

1− 2	1− 3	4	1 1
3	8× 1	2	4
2÷ 4	2	2− 1	3
5+ 1	4	1− 3	2

124

1− 4	3	2÷ 1	2
5+ 3	8× 2	4	1
2	6+ 1	3	1− 4
3− 1	4	2	3

125

1− 4	3	24× 1	2
6+ 3	2	4	5+ 1
2÷ 2	1	3	4
1	24× 4	2	3

126

1− 2	12+ 1	4	3
1	3 3	6× 2	4
2÷ 4	2	3	1
1− 3	4	1− 1	2

127

3 (1−)	4	2 (12×)	1
4 (7+)	1 (2−)	3	2
2	3	1 (8+)	4
1	2 (2÷)	4	3

128

1 (1)	3 (36×)	4	2 (7+)
2 (1−)	1	3	4
3	4 (2÷)	2	1
4 (2÷)	2	1 (2−)	3

129

3 (1−)	2 (2÷)	4	1 (4×)
2	3 (9+)	1	4
4	1	2 (7+)	3
1	4 (1−)	3	2

130

4 (1−)	1 (8×)	3 (1−)	2
3	4	2 (2÷)	1
1 (6+)	2	4 (4)	3 (8+)
2	3	1	4

131

2 (6×)	1 (2÷)	4 (1−)	3
3	2	1 (7+)	4
1	4 (9+)	3	2
4 (1−)	3	2	1 (1)

132

4 (5+)	3 (1−)	2 (2÷)	1
1	2	4 (5+)	3 (24×)
3 (1−)	4	1	2
2 (1−)	1	3 (3)	4

133

6× 3	1	2÷ 4	2
1− 1	2	1− 3	4
2	8+ 4	1	3
24× 4	3	2	1 1

134

6× 1	2	7+ 4	1− 3
3	4+ 1	2	4
2÷ 4	3	1	1− 2
2	1− 4	3	1

135

1− 4	5+ 1	12× 3	2
3	4	2	3− 1
1− 2	3	8+ 1	4
2÷ 1	2	4	3

136

2− 1	3	16× 2	4
1− 3	5+ 4	1	2
4	1− 2	3	1
2÷ 2	1	1− 4	3

137

6× 3	3− 1	4	2 2
1	2	1− 3	4
1− 4	3	2÷ 2	4+ 1
2− 2	4	1	3

138

1− 4	3 3	8× 1	2
3	2÷ 2	4	5+ 1
7+ 2	1	3 3	4
1	4	1− 2	3

139

¹1	⁸×2	¹⁻4	3
4	1	³3	²÷2
¹²⁺3	4	⁷⁺2	1
2	3	1	4

140

¹²×4	3	⁶×2	1
²÷1	2	⁹⁺4	3
¹⁻3	4	1	²÷2
2	⁴⁺1	3	4

141

²÷4	2	²⁻3	1
¹²×1	3	4	⁹⁺2
¹⁻3	1	⁷⁺2	4
2	4	1	3

142

²⁻3	²÷2	⁵⁺1	4
1	4	²⁴×2	3
¹⁻2	3	4	²÷1
¹²×4	1	3	2

143

¹²×1	3	4	²÷2
⁹⁺3	²÷2	1	4
4	⁵⁺1	¹⁻2	3
2	4	⁴⁺3	1

144

¹1	²⁴×3	4	2
¹⁻4	²÷1	¹⁻2	3
3	2	⁴⁺1	⁵⁺4
²÷2	4	3	1

145

2÷ 1	1− 2	3	5+ 4
2	12× 3	4	1
1− 4	1	5+ 2	3
3	8× 4	1	2

146

2÷ 2	24× 4	2− 1	3
1	2	3	3− 4
7+ 4	2− 3	8+ 2	1
3	1	4	2

147

1− 2	3	3− 4	1
2− 3	1	24× 2	4
5+ 4	2÷ 2	1	3
1	4 4	1− 3	2

148

2÷ 2	4	2− 3	1
1− 1	2	4 4	6× 3
4 4	7+ 3	1	2
3	1	2÷ 2	4

149

2÷ 4	2	6× 3	1
8+ 3	8+ 1	4	2
1	4	2	12× 3
1− 2	3	1	4

150

5+ 1	4	2÷ 2	1− 3
1− 4	3 3	1	2
3	8× 2	4	1
2÷ 2	1	1− 3	4

151

75× 5	3	**3−** 1	4	**2÷** 2	**3÷** 6
3+ 1	5	**2÷** 3	6	4	2
2	**24×** 4	**10×** 5	**5−** 1	6	**3÷** 3
12× 4	6	2	**8+** 3	5	1
3	**9+** 2	**11+** 6	5	**3÷** 1	**9+** 4
6	1	**2÷** 4	2	3	5

152

75× 5	**3÷** 2	6	**4+** 1	3	**16×** 4
3	5	**3÷** 2	6	4	1
3+ 1	**2÷** 3	**80×** 4	**2** 2	**5−** 6	**8+** 5
2	6	5	4	1	3
96× 4	**5+** 1	3	**10+** 5	2	**13+** 6
6	4	1	3	5	2

153

20× 5	4	**14+** 2	6	**3×** 3	1
18× 3	2	6	**25×** 5	1	**96×** 4
3+ 2	3	5	1	4	6
1	**11+** 6	**36×** 3	4	**3−** 2	5
4 4	5	**7+** 1	3	**3÷** 6	2
6	1	4	2	**8+** 5	3

154

3− 1	4	**3−** 5	2	**54×** 3	6
3÷ 6	**3÷** 1	**80×** 4	5	**2** 2	3
2	3	**5−** 1	4	**11+** 6	**20×** 5
8+ 3	**3÷** 2	6	**1** 1	5	4
5	6	**24×** 2	3	4	**2×** 1
20× 4	5	**3−** 3	6	1	2

155

1− 4	**5−** 1	6	**5+** 2	5	**15×** 3
5	**16×** 2	4	3	**5−** 1	6
2− 1	3	2	**10+** 4	**2÷** 6	**6+** 5
2÷ 2	4	**6+** 5	6	3	1
108× 3	6	1	**10×** 5	**2÷** 4	2
6	**8+** 5	3	1	2	**4** 4

156

48× 4	**11+** 6	5	**11+** 3	1	2
6	2	**16×** 4	1	5	**3÷** 3
10× 2	5	**5−** 6	4	**2÷** 3	1
12× 3	4	1	**20×** 2	6	**11+** 5
6+ 1	**7+** 3	2	5	**192×** 4	6
5	1	3	6	2	4

157

24× 3	3÷ 6	2	5+ 1	4	25× 5
4	2	9+ 6	3	5	1
11+ 2	5	4	5− 6	1	36× 3
11+ 6	3− 4	1	15× 5	3	2
5	3× 1	12× 3	4	12+ 2	6
1	3	3− 5	2	6	4

158

5+ 1	3− 5	5+ 3	2	11+ 6	4 4
4	2	6× 1	9+ 3	5	11+ 6
3− 3	1	6	4	2	5
6	80× 4	5	15× 1	3	1− 2
3− 2	2÷ 6	4	5	4× 1	3
5	3	3÷ 2	6	4	1

159

8× 1	4	2÷ 3	6	25× 5	2 2
7+ 4	2	3÷ 6	2− 3	1	5
3	15× 5	2	1	2− 4	6
11+ 6	3	5+ 1	7+ 5	2− 2	4
5	5− 6	4	2	3÷ 3	1
2 2	1	20× 5	4	2÷ 6	3

160

4 4	9× 1	3	11+ 5	3÷ 2	6
3+ 2	3	3− 5	6	3− 1	4
1	1− 5	2	10+ 4	6	1− 3
2− 5	6	5− 1	1− 3	4	2
3	192× 4	6	2÷ 2	75× 5	1
6	2	4	1	3	5

161

6+ 5	2÷ 3	6	1 1	2÷ 4	2
1	7+ 2	3	20× 4	30× 6	5
3÷ 6	20× 1	2	5	9× 3	24× 4
2	4	5	3	1	6
1− 4	6+ 5	1	60× 6	6× 2	3
3	2− 6	4	2	5	1

162

15+ 4	2× 2	1	11+ 3	5	3÷ 6
6	1	1− 4	5	3	2
5	11+ 6	15+ 3	4	2÷ 2	1 1
9× 3	5	2	6	1	80× 4
1	3	1− 6	2÷ 2	4	5
2÷ 2	4	5	1	2÷ 6	3

163

3− 1	10× 5	72× 4	3÷ 2	6	8+ 3
4	2	6	3	4× 1	5
1− 5	2÷ 6	3	1	4	2÷ 2
6	3+ 1	2	10+ 5	3	4
5+ 3	7+ 4	4− 5	6 6	2	6× 1
2	3	1	1− 4	5	6

164

15+ 5	5− 1	6	6× 3	2	8+ 4
4	10× 2	11+ 5	6	3	1
6	5	1− 2	16× 4	1 1	15× 3
3+ 2	2÷ 6	3	1	4	5
1	3	2÷ 4	2	60× 5	6
3 3	3− 4	1	1− 5	6	2

165

16× 1	4	75× 5	3	2÷ 6	3÷ 2
4	3+ 2	1	5	3	6
1− 2	2− 5	3	2− 6	4	4− 1
3	5− 1	6	2÷ 4	2	5
11+ 6	3	2	2÷ 1	6+ 5	12× 4
11+ 5	6	4 4	2	1	3

166

6× 1	3	11+ 5	6	2÷ 4	2
2	1− 4	3	6+ 1	5	6 6
10× 5	2	5− 1	9+ 3	2− 6	4
13+ 3	5 5	6	4	2	15× 1
6	5− 1	40× 4	2	3÷ 3	5
4	6	2 2	5	1	3

167

6× 6	2÷ 2	1	3− 5	180× 4	3
1	10+ 4	6	2	3	5
24× 4	6	14+ 2	3	11+ 5	3+ 1
3÷ 3	1	5	4	6	2
3− 5	12× 3	4	5− 1	8× 2	6 6
2	8+ 5	3	6	1	4

168

3+ 1	2	40× 4	45× 3	5	3÷ 6
5+ 4	1	5	5− 6	3	2
3÷ 6	7+ 3	2	1	24× 4	2− 5
2	4	5− 1	3− 5	6	3
2− 3	5	6	2	2÷ 1	3− 4
1− 5	6	1− 3	4	2	1

169

4× 1	2	**12+** 3	**15+** 4	5	6
2	**5−** 1	4	5	**2÷** 6	3
11+ 5	6	**6+** 1	**1−** 2	**1−** 3	4
6	**8×** 3	5	1	**2÷** 4	2
96× 4	5	**2÷** 6	3	**10×** 2	1
3	4	2	**5−** 6	1	5

170

96× 4	6	**3−** 5	**2÷** 2	**18×** 1	3
2− 3	4	2	1	**11+** 5	6
5	**6+** 1	**1−** 4	**3−** 3	6	**2÷** 2
5− 1	5	3	6	**24×** 2	4
6	**7+** 2	**5−** 1	**9+** 4	3	**4−** 5
2	3	6	5	4	1

171

3+ 1	2	**10+** 3	**1−** 5	**2−** 4	6
2÷ 6	1	2	4	**15×** 3	5
3	4	**11+** 6	**4−** 1	5	**5+** 2
1− 4	**3−** 6	5	**2÷** 2	1	3
5	3	**3−** 4	**2÷** 6	**12×** 2	1
10× 2	5	1	3	6	**4** 4

172

2÷ 2	4	**16+** 3	5	**5−** 6	1
3÷ 1	3	6	2	**1−** 5	**2÷** 4
1− 3	**6+** 1	5	**5−** 6	4	2
4	**3−** 5	2	1	**5+** 3	**2÷** 6
1− 5	6	**16×** 1	4	2	3
3÷ 6	2	4	**15×** 3	1	5

173

18× 6	**60×** 5	3	4	**3−** 2	**3−** 1
3	**48×** 2	**30×** 6	1	5	4
1	6	4	5	**9+** 3	**3÷** 2
11+ 5	**8+** 3	1	2	4	6
2	4	**11+** 5	6	**5−** 1	**15×** 3
4	**3+** 1	2	**3** 3	6	5

174

72× 3	4	**3−** 2	5	**5−** 1	6
6	1	**4** 4	**1−** 3	2	**10+** 5
3− 2	5	**3−** 3	6	4	1
2− 4	6	**2÷** 1	2	**30×** 5	3
6+ 1	**6×** 3	**120×** 5	4	6	2
5	2	**5−** 6	1	**12×** 3	4

175

2− 5	3÷ 3	1	24× 4	6	4− 2
3	20× 2	5	12× 1	4	6
5− 6	4− 1	2	3	10+ 5	1− 4
1	5	14+ 4	11+ 6	2	3
144× 2	4	6	5	3	5× 1
4	6	3	2 2	1	5

176

18× 1	6	4× 4	16× 2	14+ 3	5
3	3+ 1	2	4	6+ 5	6
60× 4	2	5− 6	11+ 5	1	9+ 3
5	3	1	6	4	2
3÷ 2	2− 5	3	5− 1	6	3− 4
6	1− 4	5	1− 3	2	1

177

10× 1	5	4 4	1− 2	3	11+ 6
2	3÷ 1	3	24× 4	6	5
48× 4	2	2÷ 6	3	20× 5	1
2− 5	6	2÷ 2	1	4	6× 3
3	1− 4	5	5− 6	1	2
2÷ 6	3	4− 1	5	2− 2	4

178

2− 4	15× 5	3	11+ 6	5+ 1	2
6	7+ 1	1− 4	5	2	2÷ 3
2	4	5	2÷ 1	1− 3	6
30× 5	3	5− 6	2	4	6+ 1
3÷ 3	2	1	7+ 4	120× 6	5
1	3÷ 6	2	3	5	4

179

80× 1	4	5	9× 3	10+ 2	6
4	50× 5	3	1	72× 6	2
5	2	5− 1	6	3	4
2÷ 6	3	3− 2	5	3− 4	1
1− 3	144× 6	4	3+ 2	1	2− 5
2	1	6	1− 4	5	3

180

3+ 2	1	720× 6	5	4	8+ 3
4− 5	1− 3	48× 4	2	6	1
1	2	2− 3	6	7+ 5	4
2÷ 3	1− 4	5	4× 1	2	13+ 6
6	5	1	4	9× 3	2
48× 4	6	2	3	1	5

181

18× 6	3÷ 3	1	10× 2	1− 4	5
3	2÷ 2	9+ 4	5	5− 6	1
1	4	5	3÷ 6	2	13+ 3
40× 5	1− 6	1− 2	3÷ 1	3	4
2	5	3	1− 4	10× 1	6
4	6× 1	6	3	5	2

182

8× 2	2÷ 6	4− 1	5	2− 3	4 4
4	3	14+ 6	3+ 1	5	48× 2
1	5	3	2	4	6
3÷ 3	1	11+ 4	2÷ 6	7+ 2	5
1− 5	4	2	3	6	1
3÷ 6	2	5	4 4	2− 1	3

183

10+ 3	2	36× 1	6	1− 4	5
2× 1	5	6	1− 4	5+ 3	2
2	1	9+ 4	5	6 6	24× 3
90× 6	3	5	3÷ 1	2	4
5	14+ 4	12× 2	3	5− 1	6
4	6	3	2	6+ 5	1

184

11+ 5	108× 6	3	2÷ 2	4	6+ 1
1	5	6	14+ 4	2	3
2÷ 3	1− 2	4	6	6+ 1	1− 5
6	3	3+ 2	1	5	4
2÷ 4	4× 1	2− 5	3	90× 6	3÷ 2
2	4	1	5	3	6

185

1− 5	4	3÷ 2	6	12× 1	13+ 3
3+ 1	15× 5	3	2	6	4
2	5− 1	1− 4	2− 5	6× 3	6
144× 4	6	5	3	2	3+ 1
6	3÷ 3	1	80× 4	5	2
3	2	5− 6	1	4	5 5

186

8+ 1	5	2÷ 2	2÷ 6	60× 4	3
2	18+ 6	4	3	3× 1	5
4	2	1− 6	6+ 5	3	1
6	9× 3	5	1	12+ 2	4 4
2− 5	1	3	4	6	3÷ 2
3	3− 4	1	10× 2	5	6

187

2÷ 3	6	96× 4	6× 2	1	6+ 5
3÷ 2	4	6	3	5· 5	1
6	3+ 1	2	60× 5	4	3
3− 4	16+ 5	3	1· 1	3÷ 6	2
1	2	5	1− 4	3	10+ 6
15× 5	3	1	3÷ 6	2	4

188

11+ 5	6	1· 1	120× 4	1− 2	3
2÷ 6	1− 4	3	5	2÷ 1	2
3	17+ 2	4	6	4− 5	1
2÷ 2	5	6	3÷ 1	3· 3	15+ 4
4	2÷ 1	2	3	6	5
15× 1	3	5	48× 2	4	6

189

1− 3	15+ 5	3÷ 6	2	4× 1	4
2	6	4	9× 3	1− 5	1
10× 5	2	3	1	4	1− 6
3− 6	3	11+ 1	4	2· 2	5
3− 4	6+ 1	5	6	14+ 3	2
1	4· 4	3− 2	5	6	3

190

15× 5	10+ 6	4	2÷ 2	1	3÷ 3
3	1− 5	6	2− 4	2	1
12× 4	1	2÷ 3	6	11+ 5	2
5− 6	3	3− 2	3÷ 1	4	120× 5
1	8+ 2	5	3	2÷ 6	4
2	4	4− 1	5	3	6

191

13+ 6	3	3− 2	5	13+ 1	4
4	24× 6	1	2	3	5
7+ 5	2	24× 6	1− 3	4	3÷ 1
2	25× 5	4	5− 1	6	3
8+ 3	1	5	4· 4	120× 2	6
1	4	2÷ 3	6	5	2

192

14+ 1	5	2− 3	2÷ 2	4	6· 6
2	6	1	3	2− 5	15+ 4
11+ 5	4	2	1	6	1− 3
72× 4	2÷ 3	6	9+ 5	3× 1	2
6	2÷ 2	20× 5	4	3	1
3	1	4	13+ 6	2	5

193

90× 3	5	**10+** 2	6	**24×** 1	**1−** 4
2− 4	6	**7+** 1	2	3	5
6	1	5	4	2	**3÷** 3
3+ 2	**72×** 3	6	**100×** 5	4	1
1	**11+** 2	4	**9×** 3	5	**14+** 6
5	4	3	1	6	2

194

4	**12×** 1	**11+** 5	6	**5+** 2	3
2	6	**1−** 4	3	**3÷** 1	**1−** 5
3− 6	**4×** 2	1	5	3	4
3	**5**	2	4	**1−** 6	**5−** 1
60× 1	4	**1−** 3	2	5	6
5	3	**5−** 6	1	**2÷** 4	2

195

2− 4	6	**5+** 3	2	**4−** 1	5
5× 1	5	**2÷** 4	3	**11+** 2	6
3÷ 6	1	2	5	3	**1−** 4
2	**16+** 4	6	1	5	3
2− 5	3	**4−** 1	**16+** 4	6	**2** 2
1− 3	2	5	6	**5+** 4	1

196

3− 5	**2−** 4	6	**3÷** 1	3	**6×** 2
2	**1−** 5	4	**5−** 6	1	3
4− 6	2	**6+** 5	3	**11+** 4	1
24× 4	**3** 3	1	2	6	**11+** 5
1	6	**1−** 3	**20×** 5	2	4
3÷ 3	1	2	4	**30×** 5	6

197

80× 1	5	4	**3÷** 6	2	**1−** 3
4	**11+** 6	1	**270×** 3	5	2
5 5	4	**1−** 2	1	3	6
2÷ 2	1	**2−** 3	5	**2−** 6	4
54× 3	**13+** 2	6	**8×** 4	1	**20×** 5
6	3	5	2	4	1

198

3÷ 3	**3+** 1	2	**1−** 5	4	**11+** 6
1	**6+** 2	3	**120×** 4	6	5
2÷ 6	3	1	**3÷** 2	5	**5+** 4
3− 2	5	**15+** 4	6	**9×** 3	1
1− 4	6	5	3	1	**1−** 2
5	**2−** 4	6	**1−** 1	2	3

199

[12+]2	4	[20×]1	5	[54×]3	6
6	5	4	2	[1]1	3
[11+]4	6	[1−]2	[2÷]3	[25×]5	1
1	[1−]2	3	6	[2−]4	5
[15×]3	1	[20×]5	4	6	[2÷]2
5	[2÷]3	6	[1−]1	2	4

200

[11+]5	6	[18×]3	[2÷]4	2	[4−]1
[3−]1	[2÷]4	2	3	[15+]6	5
4	2	[6+]5	1	3	6
[1−]3	[4−]5	[2−]4	6	[8×]1	2
2	1	[21+]6	5	4	[12×]3
6	3	1	[3−]2	5	4

201

[3−]4	1	[3−]5	2	[2÷]6	3
[2÷]3	[60×]5	[2−]2	4	[5−]1	6
6	4	3	[3−]5	2	[4−]1
[3+]2	[48×]6	4	[3÷]1	3	5
1	2	6	3	5	4
[2−]5	3	[5−]1	6	4	2

202

[2÷]6	[15+]5	4	[5+]2	1	[1−]3
3	6	[10×]5	[3÷]1	2	4
[4−]5	1	2	3	[24×]4	6
[2÷]2	4	[36×]1	6	[2−]3	5
[12×]1	3	6	[120×]4	[8+]5	2
4	[1−]2	3	5	6	1

203

[3−]1	4	[2]2	[3−]3	[3÷]6	[4−]5
[1−]5	[1−]3	4	6	2	1
4	[3+]2	[6×]6	1	[15×]5	3
[6×]2	1	[1−]5	4	[3−]3	6
3	[6×]6	1	[20×]5	4	[2÷]2
[1−]6	5	[1−]3	2	1	4

204

[5−]1	[1−]3	[10+]2	5	[1−]6	[2÷]4
6	4	[5×]1	3	5	2
[12+]4	2	5	1	[18×]3	6
[5+]3	[6]6	[12×]4	[3÷]2	1	[6+]5
2	[11+]5	3	6	[24×]4	1
5	1	[10+]6	4	2	3

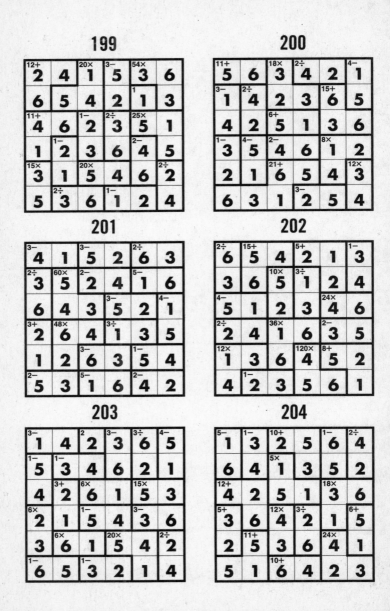

205

3 ²⁻	**5** ³⁻	**2**	**4** ¹⁶⁺	**6** ⁵⁻	**1**
1	**6** ³⁶ˣ	**4**	**5**	**2** ⁴⁰ˣ	**3** ³
6	**1**	**3**	**2** ³÷	**5**	**4**
2 ⁷⁺	**3**	**1** ⁵ˣ	**6**	**4** ¹⁻	**5** ¹⁻
4 ¹⁻	**2**	**5**	**1**	**3**	**6**
5	**4** ²⁴ˣ	**6**	**3** ⁶⁺	**1**	**2**

206

1 ¹¹⁺	**5**	**4** ⁷⁺	**3**	**6** ²⁴⁰ˣ	**2**
5	**6** ⁵⁻	**2** ¹⁻	**1** ²÷	**3** ¹⁻	**4**
6 ⁶	**1**	**3**	**2**	**4**	**5**
4 ¹⁰⁺	**3** ²⁻	**5**	**6** ³⁶⁰⁰ˣ	**2** ²	**1** ³ˣ
2	**4**	**6** ³⁶ˣ	**5**	**1**	**3**
3	**2**	**1**	**4**	**5**	**6**

207

2 ⁶ˣ	**3**	**6** ⁵⁻	**5** ¹⁵ˣ	**1** ³⁻	**4**
4 ¹⁻	**5**	**1**	**3**	**6** ³÷	**2**
5 ¹⁻	**2** ²÷	**4**	**1** ³⁺	**3** ²⁻	**6** ⁵⁻
6	**4** ⁷⁺	**3**	**2**	**5**	**1**
1 ⁷⁺	**6**	**5** ⁸⁺	**4** ¹⁰⁺	**2** ¹⁻	**3**
3 ³	**1**	**2**	**6**	**4** ¹⁻	**5**

208

3 ³	**4** ¹⁴⁴ˣ	**1**	**6**	**5** ²⁻	**2** ²÷
5 ¹⁻	**6**	**2** ³⁺	**1**	**3**	**4**
6	**1** ³÷	**5** ¹⁰ˣ	**2**	**4** ¹⁻	**3**
2 ²÷	**3**	**6** ²⁴ˣ	**4**	**1** ⁶⁺	**5**
1	**5** ¹⁴⁺	**4** ¹⁻	**3**	**2** ¹²ˣ	**6**
4	**2**	**3**	**5** ¹¹⁺	**6**	**1**

209

4 ⁷⁺	**1**	**3** ³	**6** ⁴⁻	**2**	**5** ¹²⁺
2	**5** ⁷⁵ˣ	**4** ¹⁻	**3**	**6**	**1**
5	**3**	**2** ⁴ˣ	**1**	**4** ²⁻	**6**
3 ²÷	**6**	**1** ²⁰ˣ	**2**	**5** ¹⁻	**4**
6 ⁵⁻	**2** ²⁻	**5**	**4**	**1** ⁶⁺	**3**
1	**4**	**6** ¹⁴⁺	**5**	**3**	**2**

210

6 ²÷	**4** ¹⁻	**5**	**1** ³÷	**3**	**2** ¹⁰⁺
3	**6** ⁹⁺	**1**	**2** ⁷⁺	**4**	**5**
5 ⁵	**2**	**6** ²⁸⁸ˣ	**4**	**1**	**3**
2 ³⁻	**5**	**4**	**3**	**6** ⁵⁻	**1**
4 ⁴ˣ	**1**	**3** ⁸⁺	**5**	**2** ⁴⁸ˣ	**6**
1	**3** ¹⁶⁺	**2**	**6**	**5**	**4**

211

3	4	2	5	6	1
2	3	6	1	4	5
5	2	1	4	3	6
4	6	5	2	1	3
1	5	3	6	2	4
6	1	4	3	5	2

212

1	3	6	5	2	4
6	1	4	3	5	2
3	6	1	2	4	5
4	5	2	6	1	3
5	2	3	4	6	1
2	4	5	1	3	6

213

3	2	4	5	1	6
5	1	3	6	4	2
6	4	5	3	2	1
2	3	1	4	6	5
1	5	6	2	3	4
4	6	2	1	5	3

214

4	3	2	5	6	1
3	6	5	2	1	4
6	4	3	1	2	5
5	2	1	4	3	6
2	1	4	6	5	3
1	5	6	3	4	2

215

4	5	3	6	2	1
6	4	2	5	1	3
5	3	4	1	6	2
1	6	5	2	3	4
3	2	1	4	5	6
2	1	6	3	4	5

216

1	4	2	6	5	3
6	5	4	2	3	1
5	3	6	1	4	2
4	2	5	3	1	6
3	6	1	5	2	4
2	1	3	4	6	5

217

1− 5	6	12× 4	3	2÷ 2	1
2÷ 4	8+ 5	3	5− 1	6	1− 2
2	144× 4	1− 5	6	12× 1	3
6	2	2÷ 1	20× 5	3	4
3	3÷ 1	2	4	1− 5	1− 6
1 1	3	3÷ 6	2	4	5

218

2÷ 4	30× 6	5	3÷ 1	3	1− 2
2	11+ 5	4	5− 6	1	3
3 3	3− 1	2	8+ 5	2− 4	30× 6
30× 6	4	6× 1	3	2	5
5	2	3	2− 4	6	5+ 1
1	3− 3	6	3− 2	5	4

219

12+ 2	1− 4	2÷ 1	1− 5	2− 3	6 6
4	3	2	6	5	3÷ 1
6	10× 2	5	3− 4	1	3
3 3	5− 1	2÷ 4	2	3÷ 6	15+ 5
25× 5	6	2÷ 3	3÷ 1	2	4
1	5	6	3	4	2

220

1− 4	180× 5	6	6+ 3	1	2
5	6	3÷ 3	1	10+ 2	4
5− 6	1− 3	9+ 5	2	4	2− 1
1	4	2	5 5	20+ 6	3
1− 2	13+ 1	2− 4	6	3	5
3	2	1	4	5	6

221

6+ 1	5	8+ 3	2	15+ 4	6
2÷ 2	1− 6	5	3	1	4
4	1− 3	3÷ 2	6	25× 5	1
30× 6	2	12× 4	1	3	5
5	5− 1	6	20× 4	72× 2	3
1− 3	4	1	5	6	2

222

2 2	7+ 4	30× 6	5	11+ 3	10+ 1
1− 4	1	2	3	5	6
5	15+ 6	4	2× 2	1	3
18+ 3	30× 2	5	1	144× 6	2÷ 4
1	5	3	6	4	2
6	3	1	4	10× 2	5

223

3× **3**	**1**	11+ **2**	**5**	**4**	15× **6**
1	72× **6**	**3**	2÷ **2**	**5**	**4**
3÷ **2**	2- **5**	**4**	**1**	5- **6**	6× **3**
6	**3**	15+ **5**	12× **4**	**1**	**2**
40× **5**	**4**	**6**	**3**	18+ **2**	**1**
4	**2**	**1**	**6**	**3**	**5**

224

2× **1**	**2**	9+ **3**	15+ **6**	**5**	1- **4**
3÷ **2**	**1**	**4**	**5**	10+ **6**	**3**
6	2- **5**	**2**	**4**	3÷ **3**	**1**
72× **4**	**3**	12+ **6**	6+ **2**	**1**	40× **5**
3	**6**	**5**	**1**	**4**	**2**
1- **5**	**4**	**1**	**3**	4- **2**	**6**

225

3÷ **6**	**2**	2- **3**	**5**	4× **4**	**1**
2	**3**	2- **4**	2÷ **6**	**1**	12+ **5**
3- **4**	**1**	**6**	**3**	**5**	**2**
11+ **5**	**6**	6+ **1**	2- **4**	1- **2**	**3**
2- **1**	**4**	**5**	**2**	432× **3**	**6**
3	**5**	2÷ **2**	**1**	**6**	**4**

226

8× **4**	3÷ **6**	**2**	2- **3**	**1**	120× **5**
1	**2**	8+ **3**	**5**	**6**	**4**
24× **6**	**4**	4- **5**	**1**	18+ **3**	2 **2**
10+ **2**	**1**	2- **6**	**4**	**5**	**3**
3	20× **5**	**4**	48× **6**	**2**	**1**
5	6+ **3**	**1**	**2**	**4**	**6**

227

13+ **2**	20× **4**	**5**	1- **3**	5- **1**	**6**
5	1- **1**	**2**	**4**	3÷ **6**	3 **3**
6	1- **3**	1- **4**	**5**	**2**	3- **1**
12× **3**	**2**	5- **1**	**6**	1- **5**	**4**
1	2÷ **6**	**3**	2÷ **2**	**4**	30× **5**
4	1- **5**	**6**	**1**	**3**	**2**

228

2- **5**	8× **4**	**2**	**1**	120× **6**	5+ **3**
3	5- **1**	**6**	2÷ **4**	**5**	**2**
4- **6**	2÷ **3**	4- **5**	**2**	**1**	**4**
2	**6**	**1**	2÷ **3**	2÷ **4**	15+ **5**
7+ **4**	2- **5**	**3**	**6**	**2**	**1**
1	**2**	1- **4**	**5**	**3**	**6**

229

864× 4	2	6	8+ 1	2− 3	1− 5
6	3	2	5	1	4
1− 3	1− 6	5	2− 4	2÷ 2	3÷ 1
2	4− 5	1	6	4	3
6+ 1	16× 4	8+ 3	2	30× 5	4− 6
5	1	4	3	6	2

230

4− 5	1	1− 2	2÷ 6	12+ 4	3
12× 6	2 2	1	3	5	3− 4
2	13+ 6	2− 5	1− 4	6+ 3	1
1	4	3	5	2	19+ 6
60× 4	3	4− 6	2	1	5
3	5	5+ 4	1	6	2

231

24× 4	2	14+ 3	6	5	1− 1
3	1− 5	6	3− 4	1	2
6× 6	1	1− 2	2− 3	1− 4	5
1− 2	3	1	5	10+ 6	4
20× 5	2− 6	4	2÷ 1	2	3− 3
1	4	3− 5	2	3 3	6

232

5+ 1	1− 3	2	1− 5	6	12× 4
4	5 5	12× 1	6	2	3
3÷ 6	3÷ 1	3	6× 2	9+ 4	6+ 5
2	2− 4	6	3	5	1
2− 5	2÷ 2	4	3÷ 1	3	3÷ 6
3	6	1− 5	3− 4	1	2

233

1− 2	2− 4	8+ 3	10+ 1	1− 6	5
1	6	5	3	24× 4	2
2− 5	5+ 1	4	6	4× 2	3
3	11+ 5	6	2	1	10+ 4
2− 4	1− 2	2÷ 1	1− 5	9+ 3	6
6	3	2	4	5	1

234

18+ 6	4	5 5	3÷ 2	9× 1	3
5	4× 1	2	6	3	10+ 4
3	2	2÷ 6	4 4	5	1
17+ 2	6	3	120× 1	4	5
4	3	1	8+ 5	24× 2	6
1	1− 5	4	3	6	2

235

3− **1**	10× **5**	**2**	1− **4**	**3**	30× **6**
4	11+ **2**	2− **3**	2÷ **1**	11+ **6**	**5**
6	**3**	**5**	**2**	**1**	**4**
2− **2**	**4**	5− **1**	**6**	2− **5**	**3**
2− **5**	11+ **6**	**4**	9+ **3**	**2**	1− **1**
3	**1**	11+ **6**	**5**	**4**	**2**

236

360× **4**	1− **6**	**5**	3÷ **3**	**1**	13+ **2**
6	9+ **3**	**4**	10× **5**	**2**	**1**
3	**5**	**2**	**1**	**6**	**4**
3− **5**	2÷ **2**	**1**	24× **6**	**4**	2− **3**
2	5− **1**	**6**	1− **4**	**3**	**5**
3− **1**	**4**	1− **3**	**2**	1− **5**	**6**

237

6× **6**	**1**	2− **5**	**3**	2÷ **2**	**4**
1− **4**	3÷ **2**	**6**	6+ **1**	**5**	2− **3**
3	3− **5**	**2**	2− **6**	**4**	**1**
3÷ **1**	**3**	12× **4**	40× **2**	1− **6**	**5**
1− **5**	**6**	**1**	**4**	1− **3**	**2**
2− **2**	**4**	**3**	**5**	6× **1**	**6**

238

12× **1**	**6**	**2**	3÷ **3**	1− **5**	10+ **4**
60× **5**	**2**	2− **3**	**1**	**4**	**6**
6	1− **4**	**5**	2÷ **2**	5− **1**	15× **3**
7+ **2**	**3**	5− **1**	**4**	**6**	**5**
4	**1**	**6**	1− **5**	1− **3**	1− **2**
60× **3**	**5**	**4**	**6**	**2**	**1**

239

2− **6**	3÷ **3**	5+ **4**	**1**	3÷ **2**	2− **5**
4	**1**	10× **2**	15+ **5**	**6**	**3**
2÷ **3**	**6**	**1**	**4**	3− **5**	**2**
2÷ **1**	7+ **2**	**5**	**6**	7+ **3**	5+ **4**
2	**5**	2÷ **6**	1− **3**	**4**	**1**
1− **5**	**4**	**3**	**2**	5− **1**	**6**

240

3− **5**	**2**	36× **1**	**6**	8+ **3**	**4**
3÷ **2**	1− **5**	**6**	1− **3**	**4**	**1**
6	**4**	1− **3**	**2**	2÷ **1**	1− **5**
1− **4**	2− **3**	4− **5**	**1**	**2**	**6**
3	**1**	32× **4**	1− **5**	**6**	10+ **2**
7+ **1**	**6**	**2**	**4**	**5**	**3**

241

2− 6	4	**9×** 1	3	**11+** 5	**48×** 2
6+ 1	**90×** 5	3	2	4	6
5	3	6	**2÷** 1	2	4
1− 2	**24×** 6	4	**2−** 5	3	**9+** 1
3	1	**13+** 2	**11+** 4	6	5
2÷ 4	2	5	6	1	3

242

14+ 4	**9×** 3	1	**12×** 6	2	**12+** 5
6	4	3	1	5	2
720× 3	6	2	**16+** 5	4	1
5	**8+** 2	4	**12+** 3	**10+** 1	6
2÷ 2	1	5	4	6	**1−** 3
1	5	**3÷** 6	2	3	4

243

2÷ 2	**13+** 6	**60×** 5	4	1	3
4	3	**24×** 1	**4−** 5	**3÷** 2	6
2÷ 6	4	3	1	**1−** 5	**3−** 2
3	**8+** 1	2	**2÷** 6	4	5
4− 5	2	4	3	**5−** 6	1
1	5	**15+** 6	2	3	4

244

15+ 2	3	5	**9+** 4	**36×** 1	6
1− 4	5	2	3	6	**3÷** 1
5	**3÷** 6	**3−** 1	**1−** 2	**1−** 4	3
6× 6	2	4	1	3	**7+** 5
1	**7+** 4	3	**30×** 6	5	2
2− 3	1	**1−** 6	5	**2÷** 2	4

245

144× 4	6	**2−** 1	3	**17+** 2	5
6	**2−** 3	4	5	1	**2÷** 2
3÷ 3	5	**80×** 2	**144×** 6	4	1
1	4	5	2	3	**2−** 6
10× 5	2	**3** 3	**90×** 1	6	4
2	1	**2−** 6	4	5	3

246

2÷ 6	**4−** 5	**2÷** 2	1	**2−** 3	**10+** 4
3	1	**16×** 4	**11+** 2	5	6
4− 5	4	1	3	6	**3−** 2
1	**5+** 2	3	**48×** 6	4	5
15+ 4	3	**11+** 6	**1−** 5	2	**3×** 1
2	6	5	4	1	3

247

2− 4	6	1− 5	8+ 3	2	1
11+ 5	1	4	11+ 6	3	2
3 3	5	3÷ 1	2	2− 4	6
15+ 2	4	3	5× 1	6	5
6	3	3÷ 2	5	1	240× 4
1− 1	2	6	4	5	3

248

13+ 6	3	4	25× 5	1	1− 2
12× 4	3÷ 2	12+ 6	1	5	3
3	6	5	1− 4	1− 2	1
11+ 2	5	1	3	2− 6	4
1 1	4	2	6	9+ 3	1− 5
15× 5	1	3	2	4	6

249

3÷ 1	3	10+ 5	2	72× 6	20× 4
16+ 4	1	3	6	2	5
6	5	1− 2	3	3− 4	1
11+ 5	4	5− 6	1	1− 3	2
2	6 6	14+ 4	6+ 5	1	3− 3
1− 3	2	1	4	5	6

250

4− 5	2÷ 6	7+ 4	1	60× 2	7+ 3
1	3	2	6	5	4
5+ 4	1	4− 6	2	2− 3	5
36× 6	9+ 4	3	30× 5	1	1− 2
3	2	25× 5	288× 4	6	1
2	5	1	3	4	6

251

1− 4	3− 2	9+ 3	5	1	7+ 6
3	5	7+ 2	17+ 4	6	1
20+ 1	6	5	3	4	2÷ 2
5	3	2− 6	4× 1	2	4
3÷ 6	1	4	2	45× 3	5
2	4	30× 1	6	5	3

252

72× 4	6	10+ 1	5	1− 3	2
2− 5	3	4	1− 1	2	1440× 6
3	4− 2	6	1− 4	5	1
5− 1	1− 4	3	3÷ 2	6	5
6	4− 5	13+ 2	2− 3	1	4
2 2	1	5	6	4	3

253

3÷ 1	3	150× 5	1− 2	9+ 4	2− 6
5	6	1	3	2	4
2− 3	5	2− 6	4	1	2
3÷ 6	2	3− 4	1	270× 5	3
2 2	9+ 4	3	1− 5	6	6+ 1
3− 4	1	2	6	3	5

254

3− 2	5	2− 3	10× 1	19+ 4	6
2− 6	4	1	2	5	3
1− 5	2− 1	2÷ 6	3	2	4
4	3	13+ 2	6	4− 1	5
5− 1	6	5	60× 4	3	12× 2
24× 3	2	4	5	6	1

255

2− 3	7+ 5	1	10+ 4	2	36× 6
5	1	4− 6	2	4	3
14+ 6	7+ 4	3	4− 1	5	2
2	6	9+ 4	5	3÷ 3	1
3− 4	7+ 3	2	36× 6	1	1− 5
1	2	2− 5	3	6	4

256

400× 1	4	5	3÷ 2	6	11+ 3
5	3− 1	4	3− 6	3	2
4	8+ 3	2	7+ 5	1	6
13+ 6	2	3	1	80× 5	4
1− 2	5	3− 6	3	4	6+ 1
3	7+ 6	1	2÷ 4	2	5

257

24× 1	4− 6	2	1− 3	4	10+ 5
6	2÷ 2	4	4− 5	1	3
4	2− 3	5− 1	10+ 6	3− 5	2
2− 3	5	6	4	2	3− 1
5	6+ 1	3	2	16+ 6	4
40× 2	4	5	1	3	6

258

12+ 1	4	60× 5	2	2÷ 3	6
6	1	2	3	13+ 4	4− 5
12× 4	3	6× 6	1− 5	2	1
5 5	2÷ 6	3	4	1	5+ 2
60× 2	5	4× 4	1	6	3
3	2	1	120× 6	5	4

259

11+ 4	2	**2÷** 3	6	**5×** 5	1
2	3	**6+** 5	**1−** 4	1	**19+** 6
12+ 5	4	1	3	6	2
3	**1−** 6	**3÷** 2	**2÷** 1	**1−** 4	5
6× 1	5	6	2	3	**24×** 4
6	1	**1−** 4	5	2	3

260

576× 1	4	**13+** 2	5	6	**9+** 3
2	6	4	3	1	5
13+ 5	3	**7+** 6	**10+** 4	**1−** 2	1
3 3	5	1	6	**2÷** 4	2
16+ 4	**6+** 2	3	1	**11+** 5	6
6	1	5	**1−** 2	3	**4** 4

261

36× 2	6	**9+** 4	5	**1** 1	**13+** 3
120× 6	3	**11+** 2	1	5	4
5	4	3	**3÷** 2	**5−** 6	1
12+ 3	5	1	6	**2÷** 4	2
4	**4+** 1	5	**19+** 3	2	6
1	2	**2−** 6	4	3	5

262

12× 3	4	1	**13+** 2	6	5
4 4	**3÷** 2	6	**4−** 1	5	**9+** 3
17+ 6	5	**1−** 3	4	**1−** 1	2
8+ 2	6	4	5	3	**24×** 1
1	**18×** 3	**1−** 5	6	**2÷** 2	4
5	1	2	3	4	6

263

30× 5	6	**6×** 1	**2÷** 2	**16+** 4	**30×** 3
1− 3	4	6	1	5	2
7+ 6	**2÷** 1	2	4	3	5
1	**15×** 3	5	**14+** 6	2	**11+** 4
10× 2	5	**12×** 4	**2−** 3	6	1
2− 4	2	3	5	**1** 1	6

264

2÷ 2	4	**15×** 3	5	**5−** 1	6
8+ 1	**7+** 5	2	**2−** 6	4	**11+** 3
6	1	**2÷** 4	2	3	5
2− 3	**36×** 2	6	**30×** 1	5	**2−** 4
5	3	**6+** 1	**7+** 4	6	2
24× 4	6	5	3	**2÷** 2	1

265

6× 1	**3÷** 6	2	**18+** 5	4	3
6	**9+** 3	**16+** 1	4	2	**3−** 5
2− 4	5	6	**3÷** 3	1	2
2	1	5	**3−** 6	3	**2−** 4
8+ 3	**2** 2	4	**10×** 1	5	6
5	**1−** 4	3	2	**5−** 6	1

266

15+ 2	5	6	**48×** 1	3	4
9× 3	1	2	4	**120×** 5	6
30× 6	3	**4−** 5	**3÷** 2	4	**2−** 1
5	**2÷** 4	1	6	**3÷** 2	3
24× 1	2	**1−** 4	**2−** 3	6	**8+** 5
4	6	3	5	1	2

267

6× 2	1	**30×** 6	**8+** 5	3	**2−** 4
3	**1−** 2	5	**3−** 4	1	6
5− 6	3	1	**3÷** 2	**17+** 4	5
1	**1−** 4	**24×** 2	6	5	3
120× 4	5	3	**5−** 1	6	**2÷** 2
5	6	4	**1−** 3	2	1

268

30× 2	3	5	**15+** 4	1	**1−** 6
48× 4	**1** 1	**5−** 6	3	2	5
6	2	1	5	**180×** 3	4
5+ 1	4	**6×** 2	**288×** 6	5	3
90× 5	6	3	2	4	**2÷** 1
3	**10+** 5	4	1	6	2

269

1− 4	3	**4−** 5	1	**13+** 6	2
60× 6	**4×** 1	4	**1−** 3	2	5
5	2	1	**2÷** 4	**2÷** 3	6
12× 1	4	**13+** 6	2	**2−** 5	3
3	5	2	**24×** 6	4	**6+** 1
3÷ 2	6	**15×** 3	5	1	4

270

10+ 2	4	**2÷** 6	3	**5×** 1	5
4	**60×** 5	**1−** 3	2	**6** 6	1
4− 5	6	**5+** 1	4	**6×** 2	**12×** 3
1	2	**1−** 5	**5−** 6	3	4
13+ 6	3	4	1	**240×** 5	2
3	1	**3−** 2	5	4	6

271

5+ 4	1	**1−** 3	**2−** 6	**3−** 5	2
2− 5	3	2	4	**6×** 6	1
60× 2	**10+** 4	6	**2−** 3	1	**12+** 5
6	5	**5+** 1	**3−** 2	4	3
2÷ 1	2	4	5	**2÷** 3	6
3 3	**1−** 6	5	**8×** 1	2	4

272

1− 2	3	**3−** 6	**3−** 5	**5+** 1	4
60× 4	5	3	2	**18+** 6	1
3	**3−** 2	5	**5+** 1	4	6
1 1	**2÷** 4	2	**2÷** 6	3	5
5− 6	1	**3−** 4	**1−** 3	**3−** 5	2
1− 5	6	1	4	**1−** 2	3

273

8× 1	**17+** 6	5	**11+** 3	4	2
4	5	1	2	**2÷** 3	6
2	**2÷** 4	**1−** 6	5	**1** 1	**12+** 3
90× 6	2	**2−** 3	1	5	4
5	**24×** 3	4	**21+** 6	**2÷** 2	1
3	1	2	4	6	5

274

2÷ 3	6	**3−** 5	2	**5+** 4	1
480× 2	**2−** 4	6	**6+** 5	1	**2÷** 3
4	5	**2÷** 2	1	**180×** 3	6
6	2	1	3	5	4
5× 5	1	**36×** 3	**48×** 4	**13+** 6	2
1	3	4	6	2	5

275

12× 3	4	**7+** 1	5	**4−** 2	6
13+ 4	2	6	1	**300×** 3	5
1	**2÷** 6	3	4	5	**2÷** 2
30× 6	**15×** 3	5	**10+** 2	1	4
5	**2÷** 1	2	**72×** 6	4	3
3− 2	5	4	3	**7+** 6	1

276

24× 2	**2−** 3	5	**2−** 4	6	**9+** 1
3	**48×** 4	2	6	**1** 1	5
4	**9+** 6	**2÷** 1	2	**12+** 5	3
1	2	**2÷** 6	**4−** 5	3	4
1− 6	**6+** 5	3	1	**2÷** 4	**3÷** 2
5	1	**1−** 4	3	2	6

277

2 ¹⁻	3 ²⁻	5 ⁴⁰ˣ	6	1 ³⁻	4
3	5	1	2	4 ¹⁴⁴ˣ	6
1 ⁶⁺	2	3	4	6	5 ⁵
6 ¹²⁺	4	2	1 ³⁰ˣ	5 ¹³⁺	3
4 ⁹⁺	1 ⁷⁺	6	5	3	2
5	6	4 ¹⁻	3	2 ²÷	1

278

1 ⁵⁻	6	3 ⁶⁰ˣ	5	4	2 ¹¹⁺
6 ³÷	3 ³÷	1	2 ³⁻	5	4
2	1 ³⁻	4 ²⁻	6	3 ¹⁻	5
3 ⁸⁺	4	5 ⁴⁻	1	2	6 ¹⁰⁺
5	2 ³÷	6	4 ³⁻	1	3
4 ¹⁻	5	2 ¹¹⁺	3	6	1

279

3 ¹⁻	4 ²⁴ˣ	1	5 ¹¹⁺	6	2 ¹⁰ˣ
2	6	4 ¹⁴⁺	1	3	5
1 ²⁻	3	6	2 ²	5 ⁴⁻	4 ²⁻
4 ²÷	2	5 ⁷²⁰ˣ	3	1	6
5 ¹⁻	1 ⁶⁺	2	6	4	3 ²⁻
6	5	3 ³	4 ²÷	2	1

280

5 ⁷⁵ˣ	1 ⁵⁺	4	6 ³÷	2	3 ⁶⁺
3	5	6 ³⁰ˣ	4 ³⁻	1	2
2 ¹²ˣ	6	5	1	3 ¹⁻	4
1	2 ¹²⁺	3	5	4 ¹²⁰ˣ	6
6	4	2 ⁶ˣ	3	5	1
4 ¹⁻	3	1 ¹⁻	2	6 ¹⁻	5

281

5 ¹⁰ˣ	2	1	3 ¹¹⁺	6 ²⁻	4 ²÷
6 ³⁻	3	5	1	4	2
1 ³⁻	4	2	6 ⁹⁰ˣ	5	3
4 ¹⁻	5	3 ³⁶⁰ˣ	2 ⁹⁺	1	6
3 ³÷	1	6	4	2 ¹⁻	5 ⁴⁻
2 ²	6 ²⁻	4	5	3	1

282

1 ⁶⁺	5	3 ¹¹⁺	2 ²÷	6 ¹⁻	4 ¹²ˣ
2 ²÷	1	6	4	5	3
4	2 ²÷	1	5 ¹⁴⁺	3	6
6 ²÷	4	2 ²⁴⁰ˣ	3 ³÷	1	5 ⁵
3	6	5	1 ⁵⁻	4 ²÷	2
5 ²⁻	3	4	6	2	1

283

30× 5	1	**9+** 4	**2÷** 6	3	**7+** 2
6	2	3	**2−** 5	4	1
2÷ 2	**7+** 6	1	3	**9+** 5	4
1	**15×** 3	5	**2÷** 4	**4−** 2	6
48× 4	**60×** 5	6	2	**9+** 1	3
3	4	2	**6×** 1	6	5

284

1− 3	**4−** 2	6	**20×** 5	4	**3÷** 1
2	**14+** 4	**6×** 1	6	**13+** 5	3
4	6	**2÷** 2	1	3	5
15+ 1	**2−** 5	3	**2÷** 4	2	**6** 6
6	3	**3−** 5	2	**7+** 1	4
5	**3−** 1	4	**2÷** 3	6	2

285

90× 5	3	**3−** 4	1	**4−** 2	6
3	2	**60×** 6	**10+** 4	1	5
2÷ 1	**3−** 4	2	5	**120×** 6	**3** 3
2	1	**14+** 3	6	5	4
720× 4	6	5	**6×** 2	3	1
6	5	**3÷** 1	3	**2÷** 4	2

286

10+ 4	**3−** 2	5	**6×** 1	6	**12+** 3
5	1	**2÷** 2	4	3	6
30× 6	5	**1−** 3	2	**5+** 1	4
1− 3	4	6	**1−** 5	**2÷** 2	1
2÷ 1	**10+** 6	4	**2−** 3	5	**3−** 2
2	**3÷** 3	1	6	**2−** 4	5

287

1− 5	4	**3÷** 3	1	**4−** 6	2
5+ 1	**10×** 2	5	**72×** 6	4	**2−** 3
4	**10+** 6	1	3	**13+** 2	5
3	1	**10+** 2	4	5	6
180× 6	5	4	**2** 2	**9+** 3	1
2	3	**30×** 6	5	1	4

288

3÷ 6	2	**60×** 5	**3÷** 3	**10+** 1	4
1− 3	4	2	1	5	**5−** 6
5 5	**15×** 3	6	**14+** 4	2	1
1	5	**8+** 4	2	6	**2−** 3
2÷ 2	1	3	**1−** 6	**24×** 4	5
2− 4	6	1	5	3	2

289

5− **6**	**1**	7+ **5**	2− **3**	2÷ **2**	**4**
12× **4**	**3**	**2**	**1**	1− **5**	**6**
4− **5**	16+ **4**	**6**	30× **2**	**3**	10+ **1**
1	**2**	**4**	**5**	**6**	**3**
1− **3**	4− **5**	**1**	2− **6**	**4**	3− **2**
2	3− **6**	**3**	5+ **4**	**1**	**5**

290

36× **1**	**6**	**2**	2− **3**	**5**	13+ **4**
12+ **2**	**1**	**3**	6 **6**	**4**	**5**
6	**4**	10× **5**	**1**	**2**	1− **3**
11+ **5**	**3**	24× **1**	**4**	**6**	**2**
3	15+ **5**	**4**	3− **2**	18× **1**	**6**
2÷ **4**	**2**	**6**	**5**	**3**	**1**

291

2÷ **2**	72× **6**	**3**	11+ **1**	**4**	3− **5**
1	1− **3**	**4**	**6**	2− **5**	**2**
2− **6**	**4**	1− **2**	2− **5**	**3**	6× **1**
4	10× **5**	**1**	**3**	9+ **2**	**6**
8+ **3**	**1**	3− **5**	**2**	**6**	1− **4**
5	**2**	10+ **6**	**4**	**1**	**3**

292

1− **4**	**5**	18× **1**	**6**	5+ **3**	**2**
15+ **6**	2÷ **1**	**2**	**3**	3− **5**	1− **4**
3	**6**	3− **4**	**1**	**2**	**5**
10× **1**	**2**	1− **5**	**4**	2− **6**	3÷ **3**
5	3− **3**	**6**	10+ **2**	**4**	**1**
2÷ **2**	**4**	**3**	**5**	6× **1**	**6**

293

2÷ **6**	2÷ **2**	1 **1**	10+ **3**	240× **5**	**4**
3	**1**	**2**	**5**	3− **4**	**6**
20× **4**	**5**	2÷ **3**	**6**	**1**	**2**
360× **5**	**6**	2− **4**	**2**	5+ **3**	4− **1**
2÷ **1**	**3**	16+ **6**	**4**	**2**	**5**
2	**4**	**5**	**1**	3− **6**	**3**

294

3÷ **6**	**2**	2÷ **4**	16+ **5**	**1**	**3**
1− **3**	24× **4**	**2**	**6**	10× **5**	**1**
4	**6**	3÷ **3**	**1**	**2**	3− **5**
6+ **5**	15× **3**	**1**	72× **4**	**6**	**2**
1	**5**	11+ **6**	9+ **2**	**3**	2− **4**
1− **2**	**1**	**5**	**3**	**4**	**6**

295

48× 6	4	4− 1	1− 5	6+ 3	2
9+ 3	2	5	4	1	48× 6
5	1	10+ 3	15+ 6	2	4
5+ 4	5	2	3	6	4− 1
1	2÷ 3	6	2÷ 2	4	5
4− 2	6	5+ 4	1	2− 5	3

296

12× 1	3÷ 2	6	2− 4	10+ 5	3
3	4	3− 1	6	2	9+ 5
1− 5	6	4	2÷ 2	3	1
2÷ 6	3	2− 5	1	10+ 4	2
7+ 2	1	3	5	8+ 6	36× 4
4	7+ 5	2	3	1	6

297

4− 5	1	2÷ 3	6	24× 4	2
2÷ 6	1− 5	2÷ 2	2÷ 4	3	1
3	6	1	2	1− 5	7+ 4
5+ 1	1− 2	2− 4	4− 5	6	3
4	3	6	1	14+ 2	5
2÷ 2	4	2− 5	3	1	6

298

14+ 5	3	2− 6	24× 4	1− 1	2
1	5	4	3	2	10+ 6
2− 6	2÷ 4	3− 2	5	3	1
4	2	12+ 5	1	14+ 6	3
3 3	12× 6	3÷ 1	2	4	5
2	1	3	15+ 6	5	4

299

40× 2	5	4	10+ 6	3	1
16+ 1	6	2− 3	5	9+ 4	2
5	4	4− 1	2÷ 2	6 6	3
24× 3	2	5	4	12+ 1	6
4	12+ 3	6	1	2	5
6 6	2÷ 1	2	12+ 3	5	4

300

14+ 5	1− 2	1	2− 6	4	18× 3
3	6	11+ 4	5	6× 2	1
9+ 4	5	2	1	3	6
3÷ 1	3	360× 6	10× 2	5	11+ 4
12+ 6	4	5	3	1	2
2	3÷ 1	3	4	6 6	5

Scratch Paper

Scratch Paper

Scratch Paper

Scratch Paper